ROMAN DINING

T0303326

ROMAN
Dining

A SPECIAL ISSUE OF
American Journal of Philology

EDITED BY
Barbara K. Gold
& John F. Donahue

The Johns Hopkins University Press
Baltimore

©2005 The Johns Hopkins University Press
All rights reserved. Published 2005
Printed in the United States of America on acid-free paper
2 4 6 8 9 7 5 3 1

The Johns Hopkins University Press
2715 North Charles Street
Baltimore, Maryland 21218-4363
www.press.jhu.edu

Library of Congress Control Number: 2005923861

A catalog record for this book is available from the British Library.

For more information about the *American Journal of Philology*, please see:
www.press.jhu.edu/journals/american_journal_of_philology/

To the Memory of

JOHN HAUGHTON D'ARMS
Teacher, Scholar, Classicist, Friend
1934–2002

CONTENTS

PREFACE

WITH THIS ISSUE of the *American Journal of Philology* (124.3), we present our third special volume. This sometime series began in 1999 (120.1) with a historical issue devoted to the *Senatus Consultum de Cn. Pisone Patre* and continued in 2002 with an issue on Greek comedy, "Performing/Transforming Aristophanes' *Thesmophoriazousai*" (123.3). In the present volume, we move to a group of articles that take as their theme the important and timely topic of Roman dining. These articles are excellent examples of the interesting kinds of interdisciplinary work done by classicists who employ a variety of different approaches and use evidence and forms of analysis from many diverse fields in order to analyze Roman cultural and material practice. In a departure from our previous foci (in special issues) on history and literature, the authors here use, in addition, art history and cultural/material approaches in order to try to understand this complex social phenomenon.

It is our hope that the articles in this volume will add to the considerable biography that has recently emerged on commensality (a word much used within) in ancient Rome. Several of the articles had their beginnings as papers at a panel jointly sponsored by the APA and AIA at the 2002 APA/AIA meetings. I would like to thank John Donahue of the College of William and Mary, the organizer of that panel and co-editor of this volume, for his hard work, both organizational and intellectual.

We dedicate this volume to John D'Arms, who published widely on various aspects of Roman dining and social history and who would have been an important part of both the 2002 panel and this volume but for his untimely death. Each of us knew him in some capacity—as teacher, fellow scholar, friend, and strong proponent of the Classics and Humanities in his role as President of the American Council of Learned Societies—and have benefited enormously from his influence on our discipline.

BARBARA K. GOLD
HAMILTON COLLEGE
e-mail: bgold@hamilton.edu

INTRODUCTION

THE PRESENT SPECIAL ISSUE of the *American Journal of Philology* takes as its focus dining in the Roman world. It grew out of the APA/ AIA Joint Panel on that subject, which was part of the annual meeting held in Philadelphia in 2002. The topic is both timely and engaging. Indeed, owing largely to its perishability, its diversity, and the ease with which it can be manipulated for any number of social or political ends, food has proven to be an especially amenable topic for scholarly analysis of all sorts. The articles gathered in this special issue further illuminate the nature and function of this elemental yet highly complex social practice, offering a variety of approaches—historical, sociological, literary, cultural, and material—to food and dining in the Roman world.

In the first article, "The Way We Used to Eat: Diet, Community, and History at Rome," Nicholas Purcell shows clearly that food and dining can be profitably approached from a cultural perspective. Here, Purcell explores Roman self-consciousness about nutrition and the way in which diet (and implicitly agriculture) were transformed into a narration of historical change. The process is evident in the "comestible historiography" of the elder Pliny, in which the simple foods associated with earlier Roman history provide insight into the ways in which the Romans thought about time and change by focusing on food. Especially influential in this type of approach was Varro and, before him, Dicaearchus. Thus for the Romans, food played a notable role in the relationship of the present to various pasts; in the process it becomes an important marker in helping us to map the intellectual and cultural history of the Republican period.

Turning to Roman literature, John Wilkins, in "Land and Sea: Italy and the Mediterranean in the Roman Discourse of Dining," reminds us that Roman dining was linked both to the ideology of the early Imperial period and to the mythography of the agricultural base of Republican politics. The result is a body of texts that moralize against luxury and excess, however much this viewpoint may be at odds with actual Roman practice. In a refreshing departure from the Latin texts that typically treat these themes, the author points to the Greek writers of the second century C.E., namely, Athenaeus and Galen. Both were interested in eating and dining, but from a much broader perspective than the moralizing approach typical of so much of Roman dining literature.

While approaches of this sort help to illuminate both the universality of the dining experience and its uniquely Roman aspects, the sharing of food also intersects in interesting ways with gender and the body. Matthew Roller, in his article "Horizontal Women: Posture and Sex in the Roman *Convivium*," examines literary texts, Roman urban funerary monuments, and Campanian wall painting in order to understand more completely the complexities of female posture at Roman *convivia*. On a historical level such evidence argues for women assuming a reclining posture; on an ideological level, the reclining woman symbolizes many of the same things that a reclining posture symbolizes for men—*otium*, privilege, and pleasure. Even so, the matter of female sexual propriety is never far below the surface, especially in the non-literary sources.

John Donahue, in "Toward a Typology of Roman Public Feasting," examines public banqueting during the Principate against the background of modern typologies of commensality in order to understand not only the form but also the deeper social function of public dining. Donahue assembles a wide cross section of Roman *testimonia* and weaves them into a coherent (if imperfect) framework of festal typologies, while employing a cross-cultural and interdisciplinary approach, in this instance from French sociology. The Roman evidence is categorized into useful typologies, which, in turn, enrich our understanding of public dining and its place in Roman daily life.

Not to be overlooked within the Roman festal landscape were servants, the "human props" of the elite-sponsored banquet, as John D'Arms appropriately characterized them.[1] Here, in the final entry, Katherine M. D. Dunbabin, in "The Waiting Servant in Later Roman Art," explores the visual emphasis placed on the waiting servant in Roman society in both domestic and funerary settings during the third

---

[1] J. H. D'Arms, "Slaves at Roman *Convivia*." In W. J. Slater ed., *Dining in a Classical Context* (Ann Arbor: University of Michigan Press, 1991), 171.

and fourth centuries C.E., when the evidence is most substantial. Notable, and consistent with the literary testimony, is the emphasis on the physical beauty of these servants, particularly their long hair and beautiful complexions. Such evidence indicates a much greater concern with the visual presentation of the "private" realm in late antiquity than in the first and second centuries, and it gives us a glimpse of the aspirations of those provincials who commissioned these works.

Finally, this volume is dedicated to the memory of John H. D'Arms. His life-long interests in Roman social and cultural history first emerged in a classic study of life around the Bay of Naples, and thereafter in an equally important work on the predominant Roman attitudes toward trade and commerce in the late Republic and early Empire.[2] Later, he turned his attention to food and drink, producing a series of works that, through their keen analysis of the subtleties of Roman social relations and careful use of comparative evidence, served to introduce eating and drinking as a legitimate topic of inquiry within Roman cultural and material studies. Teacher, scholar, and national spokesperson for classics and the humanities, he had kindly offered to serve as moderator and respondent for the panel that gave rise to the present volume before illness struck. We hope that these papers in some small way serve to honor a man whose many remarkable talents were exceeded only by his willingness to share them so generously with his colleagues.

JOHN F. DONAHUE
THE COLLEGE OF WILLIAM AND MARY
e-mail: jfdona@wm.edu

---

[2] J. H. D'Arms, *Romans on the Bay of Naples: A Social and Cultural Study of the Villas and Their Owners from 150 B.C. to A.D. 400* (Cambridge: Harvard University Press, 1970); *Commerce and Social Standing in Ancient Rome* (Cambridge: Harvard University Press, 1981).

THE WAY WE USED TO EAT:
DIET, COMMUNITY, AND HISTORY AT ROME

NICHOLAS PURCELL

Abstract. Changes in foodways were an object of literary reflection on the Roman past in the early empire. They offered a rich set of ingredients with which to characterize social, economic, and cultural change. Varro is prominent in attesting and shaping this tradition, but it is an older, and more broadly based means of narrating Roman social history. Varro developed this material in his treatise, *On the Life of the Roman People*, which adapted the *Life of Greece* of Dicaearchus of Sicilian Messene, written at the beginning of the Hellenistic period. This article argues that Roman ideas of cultural and social history already took an interest in changing foodways at this time. The production, preparation, and consumption of food raised ethical and economic questions common to the milieu of Dicaearchus and to Rome in the age of the first conquest of Italy.

INTRODUCTION

IN THE HISTORY OF DIET AT ROME from the seventh century B.C.E. to the end of the Republic, there were no doubt major changes and discontinuities. The study of foodways, moreover, cannot be separated from the study of production, so that these dietary changes should track a rapidly changing agrosystem. This paper is not, however, primarily about these realities, but about *mentalités* as they are reflected in themes in Roman literature, and it attempts to show that texts about food are both less and more useful than they can appear to be in the standard modern accounts of Roman diet. Rather than what actually changed in Roman nutritional patterns, I want to trace the self-consciousness of Romans about nutrition and the way that diet, and implicitly agriculture, were made into a way of narrating historical change, especially at Rome. The object of the research was twofold. One target was Roman popular culture—those reactions and values that genuinely united Romans of different statuses—and the light that it might shed on that perennially

1

tricky issue, Roman-ness. The other was the development and uses of a sense of passing historical time in a society where historiography was for long even more rarefied a freak of high literature than it was in Greece.[1]

Thus, when the antiquarian Verrius Flaccus, in the Augustan period, says to us through Pliny that the Roman people (*populus Romanus*) had lived on *far* (emmer, the husked wheat *Triticum dicoccum*) for their first 300 years, it is not the nature of the diet of Rome in the period 750–450 B.C.E. that primarily interests me, but the idea of a 300-year-long phase in social history, the perception that there was a change in 450 B.C.E., what Verrius and his Augustan readers imagined the change to be, and the attitude to the Roman past that seeing it through the bread-oven reveals.[2]

Attitudes to food had a history, too. This diachronic theme is often obscured by treatments that construct a synoptic picture of the social construction of food in Hellenic or Roman culture, or sometimes even across the whole continuum of both. We are inclined to expansive generalizations, as when we claim that the acorn was "linked by the Greeks and Romans with primitivism." Well, yes: but which notions of primitivism, where were they first articulated, when and why did they become normative, how widely diffused were they? We can attest acorn-eating as a topos of primitivism, sure enough, in both Greek and Latin texts. But primitivism was a notion shaped and deployed in many different ways, and for which many different foodways were used as a symbol. The acorn is now understood better as a real foodstuff, thanks to detailed study of its nutritional potential (Mason 1995). Its image and associations will likewise benefit from a more finely subdivided analysis of those "links with primitivism."

There is a problem, too, with the phrase that opened the last paragraph: "attitudes to food." The tangled threads between real people in real Roman streets and complex literary representations take a great deal of unpicking.[3] I am very keen to find common ground, or at least bridges and crossovers, between the world of élite literature and actual *mentalités*, and not just the *mentalités* of the literary milieu itself. In the passage of Verrius already cited, what precisely did he—or Pliny in quoting him—understand by *populus Romanus*?

---

[1] For some preliminary thoughts on the latter problem, Purcell 2003.

[2] Pliny, *HN* 18.62: "populum Romanum farre tantum e frumento CCC annis usum Verrius tradit." For early Roman cereal-choices, Ampolo 1980 and 1984.

[3] For a splendid example, the excursus on garlic starting from Horace's Third Epode, Gowers 1993, 289–310.

But this investigation of the place of food in the history of Roman historical consciousness has wider implications. Historical consciousness is one strand in a wider social cognition, and through it we may hope to discern some of the characteristics of another elusive subject, the changing nature of Roman culture. Food has a reasonably normal place in studies of Roman culture, but all too often in the rather unilluminating *Alltagsgeschichte* or "Daily Life" studies of the Friedländer/Carcopino model.[4] By interposing history in the process, and looking at the place of thinking about time through thinking about food, we may be able to tie the collection of information about foodways to somewhat larger themes in cultural history. We may be encouraged in doing this by the fact that a historical understanding of foodways appears to have played an important part in the formation at the end of the fourth century B.C.E. of the first generalizations about these matters that we find in antiquity in the thought of Dicaearchus of Sicilian Messene.

This is a very large topic, and the treatment here cannot pretend to any sort of completeness of coverage. It is intended to open questions by presenting a selection of relevant material and to prepare the way for further work.

COMESTIBLE HISTORIOGRAPHY

In his great set-piece on the agricultural virtues of early Rome at the beginning of Book 18, the elder Pliny characteristically mixes together a rich palette of themes: piety, simplicity, and morality, but also fertility and economy. The low cost of food in early Rome gave a pleasantly Vespasianic touch to his picture: from Varro he quotes food prices of 250 B.C.E.: 1 *as* for 1 *modius* (8.62 litres) of emmer, 1 *congius* (a little over 3 litres) of wine, 30 lb. figs, 10 lb. oil, and 12 lb. meat (at about 323 g to the pound).[5] Let us begin with a quartet of celebrated dietary simplicities from the

---

[4] Above all Friedländer 1921–23. Work of this kind in the first half of the twentieth century often provided a vehicle for unconcealed cultural preferences: Carcopino 1941, 262–74 (French first edition 1939), with Arab comparisons for Roman excess; Paoli 1963, 86–91 (Italian first edition 1942), with disgust at Roman diet illustrated from contemporary ethnology.

[5] *HN* 18.6–24 at 17: "M. Varro auctor est, cum L. Metellus in triumpho plurimos duxit elephantos, assibus singulis farris modios fuisse, item vini congios ficique siccae pondo XXX, olei pondo X, carnis pondo XII." The prices were perhaps recorded as those for goods purchased by Metellus for distribution at his triumphal banquets.

Romans' account of their happier early days, taking these prices as our cue.

A Modius *of Emmer*

There is, of course, no doubt either that a very considerable part of normal diet throughout the ancient Mediterranean was composed of cereals or that this was reflected in the centrality of cereal terminology to the semiotics of ancient food systems.[6] In three ways, however, cereal orientation turns out to be more complex than one might at first suppose. First, cereals are so central that—perversely—the non-cereal complement (beans, or chestnuts, or wine, or whatever foodstuffs locally made up the bipartite Mediterranean diet) might take on a highly prominent role in social identification. Second, it was actually normal within most regions to make use of a large variety of cereal types, even when one was culturally dominant, to avoid the perils of dependence on a single crop, and to respond to micro-local environmental differences (Horden and Purcell 2000, chap. 6). Third, under the overarching sense of belonging, which defining yourself as a civilized cereal-eater offered, this variety of cereals encouraged the use of *differing* cereal species and culinary preparations of their produce as ways of articulating social separation. Fourth, it was not just the grain but the way in which you preferred to prepare it that might be the symbolically significant element.

All that said, cereals were a potent community identifier.[7] There are many examples: the one that naturally concerns us most is the claim that we have already encountered that the early Romans had depended on emmer (*far*), not wheat or barley, and that this was consumed as porridge (*puls*).[8] Pliny offers essentially etymological arguments:

> Emmer was the first food of the ancient inhabitants of Latium, and the offerings of emmer . . . are a strong confirmation. That emmer porridge, rather than bread, was the staple of the Romans (*vixisse Romanos*) for a

[6] Recently, Silvestri 1999, 347–55, for Sumerian origins of the classic Mediterranean bread-wine polarity.

[7] Aelian, *VH* 3.39; Nenci 1989; Nenci 1999, foxtail millet (*Setaria italica*) associated with Pontus and Thrace, with the Po valley, and with Elymian Sicily. On *maza/polenta* vs. *puls*, Braun 1995, 28–32; Sancisi-Weerdenburg 1995, 287, for the clash between simple and luxurious stereotypes of Persian food.

[8] For *puls* in ritual, Festus 285 L.

long period is clear from the use still today of the term *pulmentaria* (condiments); and Ennius, a very early poet, in a description of the starvation during a siege, speaks of fathers snatching the *offa* from their crying children. Even today, traditional religious rites, including birthdays, are celebrated with *puls fitilla*. *Puls* appears, moreover, to be as unfamiliar in the Greek world as *polenta* is in Italy.[9]

The phrase "staple of the Romans," literally, "the Romans lived on" (*vixisse Romanos*), should not be taken for granted. It has become standard English: but to say that a people drew life from a comestible that was a principal staple is a hyperbolic metaphor and one of considerable significance for patterns of ancient thought.

Far was the Roman equivalent of barley in Greece, and its preparation, as *offa* or more normally as *puls*, was equally distinctive. It was the latter that gave the Romans their word for the dietary complement, *pulmentarium*, the thing you put with your *puls*, though no particular example of such an accompaniment became a classic element in the Roman food system. There was a clear sense, moreover, that some grains were better than others, and this is to some extent reflected in the actualities of selection, preference, and obsolescence as far as they can be gauged from the archaeological record: the key properties are ease in harvesting, threshing, grinding, and cooking, though this is not usually explicit in ancient texts. In being emmer-eaters, the early Romans were patently adhering to a less attractive diet as well as a distinctive one. Valerius Maximus offers, as so often, a classic statement: the early Romans were so much more interested in moderation that they consumed more *puls* than bread.[10]

The historicizing perspective is very prominent in this account. The second-century B.C.E. historian Cassius Hemina, starting no doubt from the same sense of the antiquity of the use of emmer as was implied by its

---

[9] Pliny, *HN* 18.83–4: "[far] primus antiquis Latii cibus, magno argumento in adoriae donis, sicuti diximus. pulte autem, non pane, vixisse longo tempore Romanos manifestum, quoniam et pulmentaria hodieque dicuntur et Ennius, antiquissimus vates, obsidionis famem exprimens offam eripuisse plorantibus liberis patres commemorat. et hodie sacra prisca atque natalium pulte fitilla conficiuntur, videturque tam puls ignota Graeciae fuisse quam Italiae polenta." This last, confusingly, is barley porridge, Greek *alphita*, and for all its unfamiliarity, Pliny refers to it by a *Latin* name. For Ennius' context (the siege of Rome by Lars Porsenna) Skutsch 1985, 610–11. See also Ovid, *Fasti* 2.519–20; 6.180; Juvenal 14.171.

[10] Valerius Maximus 2.5.5: "erant adeo continentiae adtenti ut frequentior apud eos pultis usus quam panis esset."

use in religious rites, attributed the practice of parching the grains to King Numa, in a context that bound this basic act of food preparation both to the heart of Roman sacrificial practice and to the organization of the agrarian countryside. Numa was also said—in a more rationalistic version—to have prescribed parched emmer out of a concern for health.[11] But the problem with such a historical account is that it makes essential an explanation of how and when things changed, and here the evidence was difficult to handle. Abundance of one kind of emmer, *ador*, was seen as the measure of every kind of excellence and the indicator of status and civic esteem in early Rome.[12] This is a notable social historical argument, addressing a genuine problem about the workings of a distant society, and perhaps a rather good one, on the analogy of the *pentakosio-medimnoi* at Athens. Varro's mid third-century price list still has a prominent place for *far*. For Pliny, Ennius' account of the late sixth century, written around 180 B.C.E., has authority.

Verrius Flaccus, however, as we saw (n. 2), recorded a change in 450 B.C.E. or so. What did he have in mind? The answer must be that the Romans believed that, during the fifth century, they had needed to rely on purchases and gifts of cereals from Etruria, other parts of west-central Italy, especially from Campania, and eventually from Sicily; and these cereals will have been barley and above all wheat.[13] For Pliny, "Italy" (and he means Magna Graecia) was already a wheatland in the second quarter of the fifth century B.C.E., and he translated a line of Sophocles' *Triptolemus* (468 B.C.E., fr. 600 Radt) to prove it.[14] In these beliefs, they were probably basically correct, even though the change in cereal-type is a matter of delicate and anxious cultural construction. Not only are these

---

[11] Pliny, *HN* 18.7–8: "Numa instituit deos fruge colere et mola salsa supplicare atque, ut auctor est Hemina, far torrere, quoniam tostum cibo salubrius esset, id uno modo consecutus, statuendo non esse purum ad rem divinam nisi tostum. is et Fornacalia instituit farris torrendi ferias et aeque religiosas Terminis agrorum."

[12] The *dona adoriae*: as etymology of *gloria*, and reward for generals: Horace, *Odes* 4.4.41; Festus 3 L; Pliny, *HN* 18.8.

[13] The evidence is conveniently collected by Frederiksen 1984, 163–66, arguing strongly for the basic historicity of the change; see also Garnsey 1988, 167–81.

[14] *HN* 18.65: "haec fuere sententiae Alexandro Magno regnante, cum clarissima fuit Graecia atque in toto orbe terrarum potentissima, ita tamen ut ante mortem eius annis fere CXLV Sophocles poeta in fabula Triptolemo frumentum Italicum ante cuncta laudaverit, ad verbum tralata sententia: et fortunatam Italiam frumento serere candido. quae laus peculiaris hodieque Italico est; quo magis admiror posteros Graecorum nullam mentionem huius fecisse frumenti."

places where the new grains grew not Roman; they were, or they came to be, proverbial for un-Roman indulgences of every kind. The Romans needed Demeter and her crops; they also got Dionysus and his. Over the years from 509 to 202 B.C.E., they took a great many cultural novelties from these same places—Etruria, Campania, Sicily—never without a sense of threat and loss. The latter two are the archetypes of Bad Influence on Rome before its exposure to the corruptions of the Hellenistic world. By the time of Plautus this had become, of course, a joke. Providing better evidence than Pliny for Roman popular culture, he shows us that *puls* is part of Roman self-consciousness already by the first quarter of the second century. *Puls*-eating is attributed to barbarians or made into a mock-grandiose Greek compound name, "Fitzporridgevore" (Pultiphagonides).[15]

We are witnessing in the later reflections on Roman dietary history the emergence and mutation of a Roman sense of identity, in which a way of signifying the foodways of a single people is gradually changed into part of the Roman bid to have a cultural identity that is not just equivalent to Egyptian or Elymian or Thracian, but up there with "Hellenic" as a whole type of civilization. The elder Pliny's vision is (as often) determinedly Roman. From his Greek sources he draws comparative cultural details, which underlie his comparison of grain varieties: he allows barley to be the ancient characteristic of Greece (Pliny, *HN* 18.63–70, 72). Certain crops are made ethnographically specific, in what is implied to be an immemorial fashion, but the main use to which cereal classification is put is representing the difference between Hellenic and Roman (and we should observe that this is indeed construction on his part, choosing to describe these cultural affiliations in the way that others had described the customs of more circumscribed societies, much more reasonable subjects for this kind of taxonomy). Roman writers used cereals and cereal-products to delineate the highly fragmented cultural map of Italy before the Romans.[16]

Something similar appears in the Roman account of the history of breadmaking at Rome. The early Romans made their own bread, a task for the women of the household: albeit (of course) with emmer (Braun 1995, 34–37). Inconveniently early attestations of the word "baker" were etymologized away: it was alleged that the word really meant "emmer-pounder." Or, if it was thought implausible that the élite had made their

---

[15] Plautus, *Mostellaria* 828: "pultiphagus barbarus"; *Poenulus* prol. 54: Pultiphagonides.
[16] For instance, the Sabine *lixulae* and *similixulae*, Varro, *Ling.* 5.107.

own bread, the answer was that bread could be made for them by cooks
hired to order from the Macellum (they did not have slave-cooks of their
own). Things changed for the worse in the mid second-century B.C.E.[17]
The contortions here (of a type to which we shall return) are all too
evident: there was considerable evidence available, but it was hard to
make fit the model that was required. Into the story, moreover, there now
enters a character who will play a significant part: the Provision Market
of Rome, a development of the third century B.C.E., probably on the
model of the unsuitable economies of Campania or Sicily, from which
the name may be derived. In Varro's Menippean satire on changing
customs, *Bimarcus*, the prospect of an outraged Jupiter's smiting the
central tholos of the Macellum with a thunderbolt was envisaged.[18] Cereal economies in the Mediterranean are hard to keep bounded: they
map identity, but they also track the interdependences that threaten it.

A Congius *of Wine*

Ethnic character for the Greeks and Romans was of course especially
clearly revealed in the alcoholic beverage of choice, and that (as they
knew well) is an economic datum and not a merely cultural one. The
ancients were well aware of the significance of the *symposion*. Here
more squirming by Roman cultural historians is on view. Romans wanted
to be fully part of the civilized symposiastic world but resisted the libidi-
nous associations of vinous excess.[19] The cult of Dionysus, Liber Pater,
posed acute problems for Roman systems of religious propriety and
social order (Raaflaub 2000; Koortbojian 2002). The excellence of Italian
wine had to be proclaimed, but this could hardly be squared with the
visions of early Italic austerity. Wine is tremendously important but has

---

[17] Pliny *HN* 18.107–8: "pistores Romae non fuere ad Persicum usque bellum annis
ab urbe condita super DLXXX. ipsi panem faciebant Quirites, mulierumque id opus
maxime erat, sicut etiam nunc in plurimis gentium. artoptas iam Plautus appellat in fabula,
quam Aululariam inscripsit, magna ob id concertatione eruditorum, an is versus poetae sit
illius, certumque fit Atei Capitonis sententia cocos tum panem lautioribus coquere solitos,
pistoresque tantum eos, qui far pisebant, nominatos. nec cocos vero habebant in servitiis,
eosque ex macello conducebant." See above all Ampolo 1986, especially on the significance
of the *weight* of bread.

[18] Varro, *Bimarcus* (Nonius 180.13 and 448.18) p. 108 Riese, fragments 66–67 and 69
Cèbe. De Ruyt 1983, 246–50.

[19] For some of these difficulties with wine, see Purcell 1994.

terrible effects, graphically described by Pliny in a remarkable set-piece (Pliny, *HN* 14.137–42). We observe that in this account, by contrast with that of cereals, the viticultural achievements of Magna Graecia and Sicily (on which Vandermersch 1994) count for nothing.

The health-giving contribution of wine to life (and again we should note the significance of the claim to making existence, living, possible) is part of the solution; so is historicizing the change, through the recent developments of Italian viticulture and the contribution to taste made by Julius Caesar's triumph. Viticulture was not part of the early Roman agrosystem.[20] Progress is thus evoked, uneasily, alongside a worrying sense of the problems of drunkenness: Pliny's project is to observe "which were the best-known vintages in the year 600 since the foundation of Rome, around the time of the sacking of Carthage and Corinth, when Cato died, and how much life has moved on over the subsequent 230 years."[21] That turning point, the middle of the second century B.C.E., saw a complete transformation in Italian viticulture: "this renown is not immemorial, but the reputation dates only from the 600th year a.U.c."[22]

He does not give reasons for the change, which we, however, can easily relate to the commercialization of viticulture and the wine trade, as attested by the proliferation of new types of wine amphora, precisely from around 150 B.C.E. For writers of the first century, it is more likely that the synchronism with Cato's *De agricultura*, itself another product of the commercial boom of the second century B.C.E., determined the date.[23] However that may be, it is noteworthy that the historiography of the Roman diet identified as a significant event another intrusion into the economy of Rome of the networks of exchange of a wider world.

---

[20] Pliny, *HN* 18.24: "apud Romanos multo serior vitium cultura esse coepit."

[21] Pliny, *HN* 14.45: "separatim toto tractatu sententia eius indicanda est, ut in omni genere noscamus quae fuerint celeberrima anno DC urbis, circa captas Carthaginem ac Corinthum, cum supremum in diem obiit [Cato], et quantum postea CCXXX annis vita profecerit."

[22] Pliny *HN* 14.87: "verum inter haec subit mentem, cum sint genera nobilia, quae proprie vini intellegi possint, LXXX fere in toto orbe, duas partes ex hoc numero Italiae esse, praeterea longe ante cunctas terras. et hinc deinde altius cura serpit, non a primordio hanc gratiam fuisse, auctoritatem post DC urbis annum coepisse."

[23] An anonymous reader points out to me that Polybius 34.11.1 provides the earliest reference both to the fine wine made "at Capua" and the distinctive tree-borne viticulture of Campania.

Thirty Pounds of Figs

Another familiar vignette of Roman ancestral simplicity is the turnip-toasting of the incorruptible M' Curius Dentatus.[24] It is one of a trio of stories from the epoch of Rome's newly won ascendancy in Italy at the beginning of the third century B.C.E., with Pyrrhus' ambassador Cineas being rebuffed by Fabricius and by Ap. Claudius. The turnip-story has Dentatus reject the bribes of the Samnite ambassadors in 290 B.C.E. while sitting by the fireside cooking turnips for his supper. We observe that the villa is, however, at Tusculum. "Our grandfathers and great-grandfathers were men of spirit, even if their words smelled of garlic and onions . . . ," says Varro in a Menippean satire, with an interesting synaesthetic slide from language to diet (Varro (Nonius 201.1), *Bimarcus* 110 Riese).

Vegetables are a quite difficult sign: are they simple and common-place or rare and luxuriantly delicious?[25] Columella on vegetable gardening uses them in a rather different register from Curius' turnips: "the cultivation of gardens, carried out without great energy or imagination by our forebears, is now extremely popular. There used to be a more general participation in formal dining on the part of the populace at large, given the abundance of milk, game and the meat of domestic animals; later, when the next epoch brought prices for feasting which matched its self-indulgence, the financial limitations of the populace debarred it from the more valuable foodstuffs and forced on it the more proletarian ones. That is the reason why horticulture now needs a fuller coverage from me than the traditional accounts—garden-produce is far more widely consumed."[26]

In other words, early Rome knew an abundance of animal products, the fruits of hunting, itself a classic symbol of primitive simplicity, and the husbandry of the small holding—*domesticae pecudes* as opposed,

---

[24] Cicero, *Sen.* 55, villa near Tusculum; Plutarch, *Apophth. M'. Curii* 2; *Cato Maior* 2.2 etc.

[25] Gowers 1993, 96–100, discussing problems with vegetables in Plautus, *Pseudolus* 810–21, acutely explores some of these ambiguities, raising interesting questions about exoticism and flavour.

[26] Columella 10.*pr.*1.1–3: "cultus hortorum segnis ac neglectus quondam veteribus agricolis nunc vel celeberrimus . . . largior . . . pauperibus fuit usus epularum, lactis copia ferinaque et domesticarum pecudum carne . . . mox cum sequens . . . aetas dapibus libidinosa pretia constituerit . . . plebeia paupertas submota a pretiosioribus cibis ad vulgares compellitur. quare cultus hortorum, quoniam fructus magis in usu est, diligentius nobis quam tradiderunt maiores praecipiendus est."

carefully, to the products of commercialized herding. Because of this abundance, all these good things were cheap; Columella uses the same index and argument as Varro on 250 B.C.E. *Far* must be the other part of this dietary reconstruction; the animal products provided the complement, and there was little need to care for vegetables. In these days *epulae* were normal for Roman citizens: he must mean that the low prices made possible a far more regular communal eating regime, on the analogy of the Spartan *syssitia*.[27] Curius' turnips were, even by early Roman standards, then, the sign of a low priority for dining, the product of a thoroughly disinterested, unprofessional approach to agriculture. He also divides Roman history into a happy age and the *sequens aetas* when refinement of taste raised prices and banquets became exclusive, creating social stratification by wealth.

The most interesting of these points is, however, the economic history of plebeian supply. Every Roman had once had a *hortus*: it is not horticulture that is new (Purcell 1996). The *hortus* was indeed once the *macellum* of the *plebs*.[28] Horticulture has latterly become a major growth area, come to resemble, indeed, much more closely, the world of the Macellum, because it supplies the huge demand for *vulgares cibi*. For Columella, a major change in Roman diet is to be attributed to the prevalence of *paupertas*, a poverty that is not the complete indigence of the desperate outsider, but a precarious dependence among the less well-off members of the community. This social change demands inclusion in an agricultural treatise because it has transformed opportunities for profitable production. The *populus Romanus* is at the centre of these changes, and the implication is that the interest in catering for the new market as well as the demand itself is a matter for plebeian interest. Once again, the history of diet revolves around strikingly economic issues.

Twelve Pounds of Meat

Columella's quietly pastoral Romans and Varro's plebeians of 250 B.C.E. all enjoyed the inexpensive meat in early Rome. We cannot but be reminded of the images of meat-eating heroes with which the Greeks pictured that earlier age of human existence and which have had such

---

[27] It is noteworthy that Varro also compared the Roman tradition of not reclining to practice in Sparta and Crete, *De gente populi romani* fr. 21 Peter.

[28] Pliny, *HN* 19.52: "ex horto plebei macellum, quanto innocentiore victu!"

bizarre effects on modern reconstructions of Dark Age diet. But it is vital
that (for all the realism with which the Greeks envisaged the Homeric
age) these are seriously historical carnivores, set in what purports to be a
historical Rome. The implication of Varro's price list is clear: there was a
market in meat. Even in Ovid's evocation of the early Roman festival
diet, where he imagines the deity as a visitor who has no taste for modern
Roman food and demands emmer and beans, cured pork is on the menu,
and Juvenal explicitly sets it alongside the flesh of a sacrifice (Ovid, *Fasti*
6.169–72; Juvenal 11.83–85). No question, then, that the Romans imagined meat as having been available *only* as a result of the sacrificial
economy.[29]

The pork-economy of second-century Italy made a deep impression on Polybius in much the same way as the Franks' taste in pork was
to be used by observers in late antiquity.[30] There is little doubt that the
Romans' reconstruction is essentially correct: silvicultural swineherding
is extremely likely to have been an ancient Italic practice. But this, too,
was an anxious area for the Roman cultural historian, with many points
of contact with the problem of the history of Roman and Italian wine.
There was an awkward contrast with Greek dietary history, and meat-
eating was hard to reconcile with serious simplicity, especially given the
possibilities of moving meat-foodstuffs up the scale of profitability and
luxury. The unease is ultimately reflected in the complex attitudes to the
regulation of meat consumption in the metropolis of the late Republic
and early empire. Varro saw a natural progression—or decline—in meat-
cooking habits, from roast, through boiled, to cooking with sauces.[31]
More specifically Roman and historical was the transmission that he
postulated for different *charcuteries* in the third century, when Roman
soldiers on campaign learned from their Lucanian or Faliscan enemies.[32]
Once again, what the real Roman people actually did is interestingly
relevant to what their precursors might be imagined to have done.[33] Certainly the gamblers who used the marble gaming-board whose spaces

[29] For the Roman meat trade, see now Chioffi 1999. Varro, *Res Rust.* 2.5.11 clearly
distinguishes purchase for butchery from purchase for sacrifice.
[30] Polybius 12.4.5–14, compare 2.15 on Cisalpina; Anthimus, *De observatione*, and
the Franks' taste for lard.
[31] *Ling.* 5.109: "hanc primo assam, secundo elixam, tertio e iure uti coepisse natura
docet."
[32] *Ling.* 5.111, the *Lucanicum* and the *Faliscus venter*.
[33] Corbier 1989 is useful on meat eating. This is a huge topic that cannot be discussed
even in outline here.

proclaimed [H]ABEMVS IN CENA PVLLUM PISCEM PERNAM PAONEM (we have for dinner: chicken, fish, ham, peacock) were as aware of these allusions and resemblances as any spectator of Plautus' plays (Ferrua 1964, 34, n. 178).

Towards the Dietary History of Rome

Food for the Romans thus plays a notable role, perhaps even a surprising one, in the relationship of the present to various pasts. Consider, for instance, by contrast, the relatively small part in modern popular histori-cal consciousness played by changes in foodways by comparison with, say, clothing or ethics. The picture so far is an intricate and contested one in which historical themes rich in nuance and allusion are playing a notably complex role. Lowell Edmunds was right to note (Edmunds 1980) that the semiology of Roman food reposes—far more than in modern food-systems—in the ingredients. I argue that this reflects the far greater proximity of the consumer to the producer. But it follows that what can appear to be items on a list of very comparable raw materials— bread, wine, cheese, beans—should actually be differentiated very strongly because of the diverse economic and social processes that underlie each. This lack of differentiation is actually a product of the distancing of modern perceptions from the milieu of the producer, in that it is tempt-ing to think of different foodstuffs as members of a simple series—in other words, what we see on the supermarket shelf—all homogenized for our convenience. The Roman could not think of the products of animal husbandry and of viticulture as so easily seriated. The significance of the raw materials was in consequence prone to ethical treatment, but it was also—and *pari passu*—the subject matter of history. The changes that we look for in the restaurant kitchen the Romans looked for on the land.

The most obvious historiographical element in Roman accounts of their diet is the elaboration of primitive Rome and the investigation of original, primeval, explanatory, and perhaps normative foodways. Note in passing that this way of thinking establishes the normality of *change*, which is not to be taken for granted in folk historicizing. As we have noticed, what Greece does with mythology, Rome does with early history (Scarpi 1989). It makes a big difference. For Greek thought, changes in food ways are primeval, part of the origins of humanity. The Romans conceived of the changes that had happened to them as existing within a notably different kind of time, within a real history. The implication for them was the one that we should also draw: whereas it was not possible to revisit the days when kindly gods gave humans new food-plants and taught them new ways, the changes that Romans discussed might be revisited, repeated, or repealed. Instead of being part of the explanatory framework of everything, these ideas were part of a political narrative in which it was (more) possible to reverse either good or bad trends, decline or an increment in prosperity.

"That ancient progeny of Romulus and Numa," says Columella, although he actually seems to be speaking of the age of Aemilianus, "thought it a matter of high importance that if the life of the villa were to be compared with that of the town, it should not fall short in any respect."[34] Columella, too, tells us that Mago's treatise began with the ringing moral precept that the man who buys a country property should sell his townhouse.[35] Here the *vita urbana* is clearly a tool of analysis, and there are problems for Roman interpreters. There is a cultural surprise, in so Roman a maxim coming from a Carthaginian, and in the town-country pattern having so high a profile in a Carthaginian work, when Carthage was seen by contrast to Rome as a great trading city, filled with the vices that derive from seaborne commerce. But there is also a problem with Rome's own urban tradition. Theirs had been a great city already in the time of the Kings, as they rightly believed. *Vita villatica* was also very ancient. What had the balance of town and country originally been like, in that case? How had the town worked? The solution was to devise the myth of the harmless agrotown, a temporary abode for the rustic military heroes of the early Republic, such as Cincinnatus.

It was the life of this (more-or-less) sanitized metropolis that was perverted little by little through exposure during the fifth century, as the result of necessity, to the cereal economies of Etruria, Campania, and Sicily, and to the cultural traits that accompanied it. The taste for more expensive and recherché foodstuffs was one such trait; the agrarian sys-

---

[34] Columella 8.16.2: "magni . . . aestimabat vetus illa Romuli et Numae rustica progenies, si urbanae vitae comparetur villatica, nulla parte copiarum defici."

[35] Columella 1.1.18: "maximeque reor hoc significantem Poenum Magonem, suorum scriptorum primordium talibus auspicatum sententiis: qui agrum paravit, domum vendat, ne malit urbanum quam rusticum larem colere. Cui magis cordi fuerit urbanum domicilium, rustico praedio non erit opus. Quod ego praeceptum, si posset his temporibus observari, non immutarem" ("and in particular I think of Mago's way of expressing this, making the appropriate opening to his whole oeuvre with sentiments like this: 'the man who buys an estate should sell his town-house, to save him from preferring the worship of the town gods to those of the country. A man whose heart is in an urban address will not need a country estate.' A maxim which I would not alter, if it could only be maintained in our times").

tems and retail networks that provided them were another. Unease at both was encapsulated in the general opprobrium that attached to the third-century Macellum. If the periodization of this change seems slipshod, it is because the Romans themselves had great difficulties fitting the fact of cultural change into a very long span of time and in relating it to the available facts. Indeed, the Roman unwillingness to believe that much could have changed before the ancestral virtues were made patent by their resilience in the face of Hannibal has had serious effects on our understanding of the third century: the discovery of productive villas and networks of amphora distribution from before the Second Punic War should never have been such a surprise.

A sense of vulnerability to moral decline driven by economic change was already familiar at Rome by the late third century, when Fabius Pictor wrote of the Romans' "first discovering the meaning of wealth" when they conquered the Sabines at the beginning of that century (Strabo 5.3.1). It is hardly surprising that it found expression in dietary terms. In what we know of the elder Cato, in the provisions of the long sequence of *leges cibariae* (as Cato called them), in fragments of historians such as Cassius Hemina, and in Lucilian satire, we can trace a gathering preoccupation with the growth of luxury and the decline in ethical standards that was explicitly tied to the expanding horizons of Roman power, continuing the process of eroding isolation and singularity.[36] In all this, there is a characteristic interest in the experience of a certain collectivity, the Roman People, as the practitioners of dietary change, however that entity might be defined. The subject is clearly political, tensely related to debates on aristocratic lifestyle and on the distribution of wealth in society. There continues to be no agreement as to the turning points and stages of the cultural changes that are in progress. Diet-history is a subdivision of that much larger way of conceptualizing passing time, the history of moral decline and recovery; indeed, it is a way of indexing that history (Lintott 1972; Levick 1982).

VARRO AND DICAEARCHUS

Now, behind many of the texts that I have cited, we can see or infer the name of M. Terentius Varro. He was clearly the strongest of influences on

---

[36] Sumptuary laws: Gellius, *NA* 2.24; Macrobius, *Sat.* 3, 17, and C. Titius' remarkable *suasio legis Fanniae*, quoted by Macrobius 3.16.14–16; Cassius Hemina on Numa's seafood ban, Pliny *HN* 32.20.

first-century writers such as Columella and Pliny, and his ideas about food in Roman culture were also mediated to them indirectly through his successors in Augustan scholarship, Verrius Flaccus and Ateius Capito. The work in which he expressed most of them was intriguingly entitled *De vita populi Romani*, "On the Life of the Roman People."[37] This seems to suggest life as lifestyle, a way of living. But it is clear that he meant it also in the other, more basic sense of Life, lifetime, lifespan, life-history. Its contents are apparent from a fragment: "first on the household and its subdivisions; second on the earliest customs connected to food; third on the ancient disciplines which are needful for life."[38] His way into the quite complex concept of a Roman culture was to draw the analogy between the Roman people and an individual. Since way-of-life was relatively easily predicable of an individual and comprehensible as part of his character, this analogy offered a painless way of approaching the collectivity and generalizing about it. The more so since the *pars pro toto* in question was a familiar metonymy, and since there was an old and essentially political way of thinking in which the community was represented by its leading men, and the character of one, for good or bad, could be read back from the other.

A further discourse subtly intertwined here is medical. The *vita* way of thinking encouraged a history conceived as reflecting the *health* of communities. The theme of *salus/salubritas* is important also in the history of peoples in the sense of urban populations, and this theme still awaits exploration. Here it is through an essentially medical perception that time is being differentiated and the Roman experience historicized (compare Numa's concern with toasting emmer, above n. 11). But the ancients did not get far from the body in analogies of this kind.[39] Humanity had a stomach too as we see in the curious phraseology of Pliny on the social consequences of the stomach, "for the sake of which the greater part of humanity exists."[40] So did social communities. It was the

[37] Fragments collected by Riposati 1939.
[38] Varro, *De vita populi Romani* fr. 24 Riposati: "primo de re familiari ac partibus; secundo de victus consuetudine primigenia; tertio de disciplinis priscis necessariis vitae."
[39] Menenius Agrippa's famous fable at Livy 2, 32, belongs in this context too. For medical/philosophical attitudes to diet, see Gourevitch 1974.
[40] Pliny, *HN* 26.43: Plurimum tamen homini negotii alvus exhibet, cuius causa maior pars mortalium vivit. alias enim cibos non transmittit, alias non continet, alias non capit, alias non conficit, eoque mores venere, ut homo maxime cibo pereat. pessimum corporum vas instat ut creditor et saepius die appellat. huius gratia praecipue avaritia expetit, huic luxuria condit, huic navigatur ad Phasim, huic profundi vada exquiruntur; et nemo vilitatem eius aestimat consummationis foeditate. ergo numerosissima est circa hanc medicinae opera.

job under the emperors of the *curator annonae* to look after the Roman people's stomach *pessimum corporis vas* though it be.[41]

The biological analogy also entailed a conception of infancy, maturity, climacteric, and senescence on the part of peoples as well as people. It is therefore of considerable significance for understanding the great interpretative structures of progress and decline with which ancient historians and philosophers operated. Food turns out to give us an *entrée* into some very large debates indeed.

Above all, Varro's *De vita*, as it dimly emerges from the tradition which we have been sampling, was a historical account about a real Rome, however idealized the early generations were. In this it was presumably a very different work from *De gente populi Romani*.[42] That work concerned itself with origins, as Varro himself says in his *Res Rusticae* (2.1.4). Varro appears to have taken the decision at that point that for Roman purposes, he would need to separate the period of origins from the theme of the *De vita*, even if it was to be many years before he published the latter.[43]

It therefore matters quite a lot at what date we think Varro wrote *De vita populi Romani*. Does he disclose a generally proto-Augustan attitude to dietary politics?[44] Does he represent the distinctive intellectual mood of the strange years between the Colline Gate and Pharsalus? The intellectual transitions of the Roman Revolution still need more scholarly attention, and all the more so when we are dealing with figures like Varro, who almost lived to see Actium, and Atticus, to whom Varro dedicated the *De vita* (Rawson 1988, 100–104) and who lived to see Atticus' daughter married to M. Agrippa. The Roman People constituted a powerful ideological theme, apt for appropriation, overt or unconscious. One would not write about them in the same way within two decades of Sulla as one would after Caesar had won his Dictatorship. And it is certain that the *De vita* is a work of 47 or later, and some would date it to after the *De gente populi Romani* of 43 (fr. 9 Peter). It belongs in a unique moment of Roman self-reflection: one at which the pious

---

[41] Seneca, *de BV* 18.5: "cum ventre tibi humano negotium est."

[42] For the nature of the *De gente*, see above all Taylor 1934.

[43] When he did, it is not implausible to link the form it took (especially in being in four books rather than three) to the influence of the contemporary scholar Jason of Nysa, the uncle of the philosopher-historian Poseidonius of Apamea, just as *De gente* was indebted to the chronological work of Castor of Rhodes.

[44] Baier 1997: the thesis that Varro was "einer der geistigen Wegbereiter der augusteischen Epoche."

certainties propagated by a Cicero were clearly vain, and insecurity and anxiety called for the proclamation of certain Roman values; when the new relationship with Greece that succeeded the Social and Mithridatic wars was in full sway, but before these two tendencies had found their resolution and accommodation in the reinvention of Roman tradition and Roman self-definition in the *optimus status* of which Caesar Augustus was known as the *auctor*.

Another preoccupation of the *De gente*, which is inviting for the cultural historian, was what, and from which people, the Romans copied: "quid a quaque traxerint gente per imitationem" (fr. 21 Peter, Servius, *ad Aen.* 7.176). The theme recognizes hybridity as a form of self-consciousness: another fourth-century B.C.E. legacy to Rome. But at the same time such a prominent idea of complexity promotes a quite strong sense of the people as a whole: élites usually self-define as pure. Pliny has an odd exegetic category which may be related: the innovations shared by everyone (*gentium consensus*) but in all of which the Romans were late participants: alphabets, barbers, and clocks.[45]

We are fortunate to know something, though not nearly enough, about Varro's inspiration for both the *De gente* and the *De vita*. Varro opens his *Res Rusticae* with a debate on the nature of the relationship between the pastoral and the arable and makes his Romans incline to the view that they are closely related though distinct. But he emphatically cites Dicaearchus as authority for the view that pastoralism came first: "the author of this view is that most learned of men Dicaearchus, who in his *Life of Greece* [*Bios Hellados*] showed us how it was from the beginning."[46] Dicaearchus of Messene in Sicily, measurer of mountains, geographer, and philosopher-historian, wrote a *Bios Hellados* in the second half of the fourth century.[47] This is the work that Varro himself consciously imitated and adapted in composing his *De vita populi Romani* (Rawson 1988, 235). The prototype combined in a novel way characteris-

---

[45] Pliny, *HN* 7.210–12: Gentium consensus tacitus primus omnium conspiravit, ut Ionum litteris uteretur . . . Sequens gentium consensus in tonsoribus fuit, sed Romanis tardior . . . Tertius consensus fuit in horarum observatione, iam hic ratione accedens, quando et a quo in Graecia reperta, diximus secundo volumine. serius etiam hic Romae contigit.

[46] Varro, *Res Rusticae* 1.2.16: "auctore doctissimo homine Dicaearcho qui Graeciae vita qualis fuerit ab initio nobis ita ostendit." He sets out Dicaearchus' theory much more fully at 2.1.3–5. For Dicaearchus and Theophrastus and theories of decline, Dodds 1973, 16–17.

[47] Fragments in Wehrli 1944, 47–66.

tics of universal history as well as the biographical analogy.[48] It has been seen as wrestling with the invention of a theory of culture.[49] But the idea that food formed part of a set of *nomoi* that might change and be reformed is already present in archaic Greece: *agoge* in the Spartan sense might be translated "culture," for all its educational overtones. An early Athenian comic poet certainly remarked that cheese, barley-cakes, olives, and leeks were prepared for the Anakes in the Prytaneion at Athens in commemoration of the ancient *agoge* (Chionides fr. 7 K.–A.). It was Dicaearchus, nonetheless, who pioneered the way of thinking that has been so important to our analysis, the analogy of the experience through time of a people or culture to the biography of a human being, transposing the notion of *bios* or *vita* from the human person to the whole society.[50]

Certainly Dicaearchus had a strong sense of change through time and traced human society, and with it human foodways, from the days of a life in close proximity to Nature in the *Urzeit*, through a pastoral phase, and into the age of fully diverse agriculture (see n. 46). Is this a contributor to the formation of the idea of discrepant meat eating in early Rome? Only one of the few fragments to survive deals with food, but that is a fascinating discussion of the origins of apportionment, *merismos*.[51] As food shortages occurred, rules for sharing food became necessary to prevent the starvation of the weak. Dicaearchus' perspective is thus to an extent indeed a popular one, concerned at least on some level for the social justice on which community life must depend and realistic about the effects of unbridled and predatory competition. We have already noted the division made in the treatment of Rome between the historical and the mythical. In the description of Dicaearchus' contents we also see the forerunner of Pliny's interest in vanished and irrecoverable skills, and the theme *res familiaris* and its subdivisions (which we shall not have

---

[48] On *bios*-history, see Leo 1901; and cf. Clarke 1999, 40–42.

[49] Ax 2000, 349, on precursors, and especially the Palamedes-Komplex. For the differences between the Atthides and the "history of civilizations" of Dicaearchus, Jacoby 1949, 142–43. Perhaps overstated: Jacoby recognizes that Dicaearchus might have influenced Philochorus, and in attributing (133–34) to the Atthidographers an interest in the study of *nomoi* as a method for reaching back into prehistoric time, and as part of a philosophical modelling of history, he sets out some of what Dicaearchus himself might have thought he was trying to achieve in the *Bios Hellados*.

[50] For the originality of Dicaearchus' conception of change, see Momigliano 1972, 172–73.

[51] Fr. 59 Wehrli 1944 = Zenobius, *Cent.* 5.23: "sharing stops choking" μερὶς οὐ πνίγει.

time to discuss at length, noting, however, that it is another vital setting
for the discussion of food).

The comparison between the *De vita populi Romani* and the *Bios
Hellados* has a number of interesting aspects. Trivially, a claim of some
kind is no doubt represented by the fact that Varro's work was in four
books to Dicaearchus' three. The Romans needed more exegesis. But
they were also the *populus Romanus*, not an abstraction like Hellas. We
cannot, unfortunately, see much of how Dicaearchus defined Hellas,
between ethnography and geography; it must have been conceived as a
social entity in order to lend itself to the biographical metaphor. But "the
Greeks" were notoriously slippery as an ethnic category, and the apparent precision of "the Roman people" suggests another set of familiar
claims to superiority. Varro must be distinguishing the *populus Romanus*
from "Hellas," but he is naturally also adducing the majestic cultural and
historical stature of the Greek world—Rome is a system on the same
scale. At the same time, he is engaged in making claims about the central
topic of Roman politics: what *was* the Roman People, and what was its
role in the body politic?

Varro's homage to Dicaearchus was in many ways entirely characteristic of the last years of the Republic.[52] But this may not have been the
first moment in Roman cultural history to which the Sicilian thinker is
relevant. There may be something here of value for those who are interested in Roman historical consciousness in the Middle Republic, down to
the generation of Cincius Alimentus and Fabius Pictor, and even more so
of Ennius. It was not only in the generation that followed Livius'
Andronicus' *Odyssey* that Rome began to adapt to these ways of thinking. Rome was closely linked to a wider Mediterranean cultural horizon
much earlier than that. So, although it is possible that the ideas which
Varro put into the *De vita* were completely new in Rome then, or that
they only reached him by an indirect route, there are considerations that
support a more direct tie than this.

There are many reasons for thinking that Dicaearchus' milieu was
not wholly alien to that of the contemporary Rome of Appius Claudius
the Blind. It is perhaps unlikely that Dicaearchus mentioned Rome. But
the non-Greek world was far from negligible to the Greeks of the fifth
and fourth centuries. It is worth remembering the Samnite interlocutors

---

[52] For Cicero's interest in Dicaearchus, see *Tusc. Disp.* 1.77, with the very cautious
account of Smethurst 1952.

of the Italiote sages.[53] The Peripatetics, we know, were aware of Rome and informed about some aspects of its government and society. And, if Dicaearchus was more of an opponent of the Peripatos than a disciple, it is at least clear that he was in dialogue with it. Dicaearchus himself was by birth a close neighbour of the city from which was to come the first important author to attempt to integrate fully the Romans into a history of the West—Timaeus of Tauromenium—though Timaeus was considerably younger. It is in Sicily and south Italy, of course, that we should look for the centre of gravity of the world in which both Rome and many parts of what we think of as Hellas found themselves. Dicaearchus, above all, has been seen to have important links with the revived Pythagorean thought of fourth-century Italy and with the Taras of Archytas and Aristoxenos in particular.[54] Varro had Pythagorean leanings of his own (Pliny, *HN* 35.160), but Dicaearchus' sympathies will have found an audience at Rome far earlier. The interest of middle-republican Rome in Pythagoras is one of the few significant data of which we can be sure in this elusive period of cultural history (Mele 1981; Humm 1997).

Cultural stability was threatened from many angles in the late fourth and early third centuries. It was a propitious moment to model cultural change. Foodways were as vivid a sign of the vulnerability of traditional Greek culture as any other. Already for Theopompus, the sympotic customs of the Etruscan cities were a showpiece of exotic culpability (*FGH* 115 F 204). Aristoxenus had lamented the confusion of sympotic habits, *summeikta sumpotika*, of the cities that were exposed to the barbarization of Oscans, Romans, and Etruscans. A letter attributed to Plato warned of the squeezing out of Sicilian Greek culture between the Carthaginian and Oscan cultural threats (*Ep.* 8, 353; Plut., *Tim.* 1.3). And Dicaearchus' own native city was indeed occupied and changed out of all recognition by the mercenary settlers who called themselves Mamertini after the Italic wargod, and it has been supposed that he saw the terminal cultural decline of his Sicily as a reason for shifting his interpretative attentions to the Peloponnese, where things continued as they always had.[55] The Sicilian historians of the twentieth century, however, who saw this in Dicaearchus, were all too conscious of how it

[53] Cavallaro 1971–72, 221–24, however, notes the "estraniarsi di Dicearco . . . dal Occidente"; Drachmann 1912; Wehrli 1944, fr. 31.

[54] For the Letter of Dicaearchus to Aristoxenus, fr. 70 Wehrli 1944.

[55] For the Mamertini, Frederiksen 1984, 221–25; for Italians in Sicily in general, a useful survey in Tusa Cutroni 1970.

foreshadowed the eighteenth-century eclipse of their island's culture, and Dicaearchus does not seem to have been a stranger to the impact that non-Hellenic influence had had on the Greeks of Sicily. He is the author, perhaps, in the *Bios Hellados* as well as in the life of Alkaios, for which it is specifically attested, of the fullest statement of the Sikel origin of that strange Greek sympotic diversion *kottabos*, the playing of which came to be general where *krateres* were filled and *skyphoi* dipped (Fr. 94–95 Wehrli). And it was he who preserved the interesting datum for the history of the West that the rhapsode Kleomenes read aloud the *Katharmoi* of Empedocles at the Olympic Festival (Fr. 87 Wehrli).

There is also reason to think that Dicaearchus played an important part in theorizing the historicity of the age of Cronos (Bodei Giglioni 1986). It seems likely that this was for him part of the account of the decline from original felicity. Euhemerus of Messene, on the other hand, at almost the same period, in his rationalizing *Hieros Logos*, developed the narrative of Cronos and Zeus as a quasi-historical narrative. Euhemerus is a Hellenistic thinker whose thought was rapidly assimilated at Rome in the period of the second Punic War: by the time of Ennius, the west, and Latium in particular, was made to play an important part in the Cronos-Zeus narrative. In fact, cultic and, no doubt, therefore exegetical interest in Cronos/Saturn and Zeus/Jupiter is much older. The Temple of Saturn at Rome is, after all, certainly an adjunct of the Capitoline cult and certainly a construction of the beginning of the fifth century; and the association may perhaps be traced back further to Olympia in the sixth century.[56] Reflections on the primitive state of society and the nature of change are therefore inherent in Roman religion, both in this specific context and because they are inevitable by-products of a system that proclaims itself traditional and conservative. There is no reason to deny the participation of Rome in the age of Appius Claudius the Blind in the currents of thought that are represented for us by what we know of Euhemerus and Dicaearchus. The older style of argument that gave single authors determining roles in the development of culture is inherently implausible. A Heracleides Ponticus, a Dicaearchus, a Timaeus, or a Euhemerus tracks and traces cultural patterns skeined between Greek, Roman, Carthaginian, and Italic communities.[57] Their oeuvres offer narrow windows on a vastly complex

---

[56] I hope to return to this theme in a future work on the history of the Capitoline cult.

[57] For Timaeus and his milieu, Momigliano 1977b. Poseidonius is a later example of the way of thinking: see F 59, on the generalized austerity of Romans of the past ("even in

cultural world. Even if they were not so fragmentary, they would never give us the key to understanding the whole problem any more than Virgil or Horace can in themselves and taken singly offer the key to understanding Augustan Rome, a period whose cultural history is, all would agree, infinitely better known.

So it does not seem to me at all implausible to suppose that at least the Romans who fought and farmed in the Italian peninsula and its purlieus, persuaders and predators of their neighbours, in the last third of the fourth century, shared horizons and perceptions with the mentors and pupils of Dicaearchus and his congeners. We may enumerate briskly what some of these may have been.

They will certainly have approved of the economic rather than social analysis, the admiration for the active rather than the contemplative life, both of which distinguish Dicaearchus from the school of Aristotle.[58] There is no reason to think that Romans only began to construct themselves as *pragmatikoi andres* after the reception of Hellenistic literary culture. Dicaearchus' notably philo-Laconian tendencies (his *Constitution of Sparta* was read publicly every year while the Spartan system lasted) are also an interesting strand in the reception of Sparta, which undoubtedly became important at some point in Roman cultural history.[59] In particular, he seems to have been one of those who first recognized and praised the mixed constitution, yet another idea that the Romans were to make their own. As an admirer of Pythagoras, he appealed to earlier generations of Roman Pythagoreans than Varro's. There are connections yet to be traced between Greek and Roman thought that will one day elucidate how number, measurement, and new conceptions of space developed as they did in the age of the first Roman roads and the first centuriated landscapes. Finally, as a traditionalist, a *laudator temporis acti*, an exponent of ethical and historical nostalgia, Dicaearchus is among the authors whose ideas resonate in Roman thinking already in the time of Fabius and Cincius, become prominent in Cato, and are never subsequently lost. He was relatively uninterested in the Hellenistic kingdoms, which the Romans also rapidly came to affect to despise. Dicaearchus also had the interesting notion that the first property

---

our times well-off people make their sons drink mainly water and eat whatever is available"), and F 277b E–K, on ethnographic foodways.

[58] Bodei Giglioni 1986, 636; Edelstein 1967, 134–35.

[59] Rawson 1969, 82–83; for Roman Laconism in the Republic, ibid. 99–106. For Dicaearchus and Sparta, Momigliano 1972, 174–75.

had been animals, not land. Curiously, for the people whose law of property has been the foundation of all the forms of that dubious institution with which we are familiar, the Romans also had a prominent place, as is well known, for *pecus* in their narratives of early institutions.[60] Like Plato, finally, and many later Roman writers, he was an advocate of the terrestrial world in contrast to the corruption to which the sea was prone.[61]

Dicaearchus' conceptions, related as they are to universalizing history, united philosophical, historical, and geographical enquiry, and this can be observed both in the *Bios Hellados* and in the fragments of his geographical work (cf. Clarke 1999, 39–45). In the latter there is a noteworthy economic element, and it is indeed arguable that it was an essentially economic vision that underlay the development of geographical, as opposed to cosmographical, notions during the fifth and fourth centuries (Horden and Purcell 2000, chap. 1).[62] In this area, too, Dicaearchus illuminates Rome with a double radiance: his work certainly shaped Varro's influential presentation in the last years of the republic, but its ideas and preoccupations had been those of the Romans themselves, Varro's subject, since the time when the *Bios Hellados* was composed.

CONCLUSION

The recognition that discussion of *tropoi* in human society is essentially economic underlies the modelling of dietary change as we have witnessed it in the few examples presented in this paper. Underlying all the bewildering variety of contrasts and comparisons between cultures and times, the basic issue at stake is this: commercialized or not?

The Romans came to think of themselves as locked into a special relationship with the economies of Magna Graecia, articulated ever more strongly after 338 by the Roman presence on the doorstep of Greek Italy, in Campania. The cities of the Greek West—and Sybaris in particu-

---

[60] As Bodei Giglioni 1986 notes, against the view of Fustel that has reinforced the general belief in the primacy of landed property.

[61] On all these things, Bodei Giglioni 1986 is eloquent. For Roman antipathy to the sea, Purcell 1995; and on "the sea which teaches corruption," Horden and Purcell 2000, chap. 1.

[62] Dicaearchus was involved in a project sponsored by Lysimachus for measuring the heights of Peloponnesian mountains, which for Bodei Giglioni 1986, 631, is how he got first-hand information about primitive conditions.

lar—had a special place in the history of *truphe* and its antidotes, and Pythagoras is known as one of the strongest-minded philosophical dieticians of antiquity.[63] The specialized science of eating was a largely western invention, as Athenaeus demonstrates to the full (Dalby 1995). And the Sicilian theme enables us, compels us, to recall the vital place in the cultural history of the western Mediterranean occupied by another only tangentially Greek state, Carthage. It is a striking fact that the great work on agriculture by Mago the Carthaginian, translated after 146 B.C.E., began with a moral precept that is totally at home in Roman thought. Mago's work presupposes a debate about the relationship between urban and rural society, and between political and economic activities, production, and consumption, characteristic of the Hellenic tradition but clearly just as relevant to the Punic context of—at the latest—the early second century (since we know that cash-crop agriculture was prominent in the chora of Carthage as early as the time of Agathocles' expedition at the end of the fourth century).[64] The use of low prices to evoke a happier phase in ethical/economic history that we observed in the section "Comestible Historiography" (above) finds an eloquent parallel in the tradition in which Polybius used prices to illustrate prosperity in Cisalpine Gaul or in Lusitania (Polybius 2.15.1; 34.8.4).

Although the later Roman master-narrative was compelled to postpone serious moral decline to the second century, and although that age did indeed, with the conquest of the Mediterranean, bring altogether new challenges to Roman culture and society, the problem of *truphe* and its economic foundations was much older, and so was its accompaniment, real *aporia* about whether wide horizons and lively exchanges of peoples and things are good or bad, as we see it so painfully displayed in the elder Pliny. As we have already seen, he indicts *avaritia* as a major cause of human misery. His linking *avaritia* with trade and economic life does not quite take the positive shine off those things. But he has the impossible task of charting innovation and obsolescence: "for who does not think that the enhancing of global communications that results from the majesty of the Roman empire has been a good thing for human existence, with commercial exchange of goods, and the common society of a happy peace, and that everything that may have been hidden before has now

---

[63] See especially Iamblichus, *vita Pyth.* 24.

[64] Diodorus 20.8; cf. 16.83.1–2, on the revival of commercial agriculture in Timoleon's Sicily.

become commonly available everywhere?"[65] This is one of his most ringing claims for the achievements of his own times. But this remains an age when the only skills fostered are those of *avaritia*: continuous cultural change, for which he wields some remarkable phrases, e.g., *alii subiere ritus*, "other modes of behaviour have emerged"; *circa alia hominum mentes detinentur*, "people's minds have been distracted by other things." This continuous change inevitably obliterated a millennium of good practices in agriculture, which is summed up as *publicae causae mundi* (the universal operation of change in society). Cultural history is annexed to the study of the world, *nomos* to *physis*, which is of course the central paradox of the *naturalis historia*, that oxymoronic genre. It was the *vita*-thinking of Dicaearchus and his successors that provided the model and the language for this treatment of cultural history, and that is why food and its production loom so large in both.

In this anxiety, a prominent and realistic theme is political. The theme of the *populus Romanus*, nicely foregrounded by Varro in his adaptation of Dicaearchus' title, is not new in that period either. Indeed, the politics of popular maintenance and the management of community foodways are a central feature of the *polis*, already visible in the archaic period (Ampolo 1986). It is time that the *annona* were looked at from an ideological point of view as a food-system, since the debate about the *annona* must reflect perceptions of what the population of Rome could be eating and should be eating. Our subject matter is not quaintly antiquarian, but normative, in that it cannot fail to be used in defending or challenging public alimentary policy. For Gowers (1993, 17), the Roman meal (of the literary centre of gravity at which she works) itself recapitulates the history of Roman food, and though she sees this as essentially a

---

[65] Pliny, *HN* 14.2–4: illud satis mirari non queo, interisse quarundam memoriam atque etiam nominum quae auctores prodidere notitiam. quis enim non communicato orbe terrarum maiestate Romani imperii profecisse vitam putet commercio rerum ac societate festae pacis omniaque, etiam quae ante occulta fuerant, in promiscuo usu facta? at Hercules non reperiuntur qui norint multa ab antiquis prodita. tanto priscorum cura fertilior aut industria felicior fuit, ante milia annorum inter principia litterarum Hesiodo praecepta agricolis pandere orso subsecutisque non paucis hanc curam eius, unde nobis crevit labor, quippe cum requirenda sint non solum postea inventa, verum etiam ea quae invenerant prisci, desidia rerum internecione memoriae indicta. cuius vitii causas quis alias quam publicas mundi invenerit? nimirum alii subiere ritus circaque alia mentes hominum detinentur et avaritiae tantum artes coluntur. antea inclusis gentium imperiis intra ipsas adeoque et ingeniis, quadam sterilitate fortunae necesse est animi bona exercere, regesque innumeri honore artium colebantur et in ostentatione has praeferebant opes, inmortalitatem sibi per illas prorogari arbitrantes, qua re abundabant et praemia et opera vitae.

matter of a polarity between simplicity and luxury, the observation works well also for more complex narratives of nutritional change.

The eventual climax—which Pliny would have hated, though he could scarcely have been surprised by it—is Athenaeus' ahistorical panorama in which books are people and the world, summed up in Rome, a library, which served to express the indiscriminate totality of all food practices anywhere, ever (Too 2000; Webb 2000). Rome, whose food-supply managers can now claim that their business is with "the human stomach," has been dissolved into the cultural continuum of the whole world of letters, but there is still no more expressive way of displaying that continuum than in an encyclopaedic discussion of food.[66]

St. John's College, Oxford
e-mail: nicholas.purcell@sjc.ox.ac.uk

BIBLIOGRAPHY

Ampolo, Carmine. 1980. "Le condizioni materiali della produzione. Agricoltura e paesaggio agrario. La formazione della città nel Lazio (Seminario tenuto a Roma, 24–25 giugno 1977)." *Dialoghi di archeologia*, 2.1.
———. 1984. "Note minime di storia dell' alimentazione." *Opus* 3:115–120.
———. 1986. "Il pane quotidiano della città antiche fra economia e antropologia." *Opus* 5:143–52 (reprinted in Longo and Scarpi 1989, 205–12).
Ax, Wolfram. 2000. "Dikaiarchs Bios Hellados und Varros *De vita populi Romani*." *Rheinisches Museum* 143:337–69.
Baier, Thomas. 1997. *Werk und Wirkung Varros im Spiegel seiner Zeitgenossen.* Stuttgart: Hermes Einzelschrift 73.
Barton, Ian, ed. 1996. *Roman Domestic Buildings.* Exeter: Exeter University Press.
Bodei Giglioni, Gabriella. 1986. "Dicearcho e il riflessione sul passato." *RivStorIt* 98:629–52.
Braun, Thomas. 1995. "Barley Cakes and Emmer Bread." In Dobson, Harvey, and Wilkins 1995, 25–37.
Braund, David, and Christopher Gill, eds. 2003. *Myth, History, and Culture in Republican Rome: Studies in Honour of T. P. Wiseman.* Exeter: Exeter University Press

[66] An oral version of this paper was given at the University of Calgary in spring 2002. I am most grateful to Franco De Angelis for the invitation, and to the audience for their suggestions. I am also grateful to the *AJP* referees for their observations, most of which I have incorporated.

28 NICHOLAS PURCELL

Braund, David, and John Wilkins, eds. 2000. *Athenaeus and His World*. Exeter: Exeter University Press.

Carcopino, Jérôme. 1939. *La vie quotidienne à Rome à l'apogée de l'Empire*. Paris: Hachette. *Daily Life in Ancient Rome: The People and the City at the Height of the Empire*. London: Routledge, 1941.

Cavallaro, M. A. 1971–72. "Dicearcho, l'Ineditum Vaticanum e la crisi della cultura siceliota." *Helikon* 11–12:213–28.

———. 1973–74. "Dionisio, Cecilio di Kalè Akté e l'Ineditum Vaticanum." *Helikon* 13–14:118–40.

Chioffi, Laura. 1999. *Caro: il mercato della carne nell'Occidente romano: riflessi epigrafici ed iconografici*. Rome: L'Erma di Bretschneider.

Clarke, Katherine. 1999. *Between Geography and History: Hellenistic Constructions of the Roman World*. Oxford: Oxford University Press.

Corbier, Mireille. 1989. "The Ambiguous Status of Meat in Ancient Rome." *Food and Foodways* 3:223–64.

———. 1999. "The Broad Bean and the Moray: Social Hierarchies and Food in Rome." In Flandrin and Montanari 1999, 129–140.

Dalby, Andrew. 1995. "Archestratos: Where and When?" In Dobson, Harvey, and Wilkins 1995, 400–12.

De Ruyt, Claire. 1983. *Macellum: Marché alimentaire des romains*. Louvain: Institut supérieur d'archéologie et d'histoire de l'art.

Dobson, M. J., F. D. Harvey, and John Wilkins, eds. 1995. *Food in Antiquity*. Exeter: Exeter University Press.

Dodds, E. R. 1973. *The Ancient Concept of Progress and Other Essays on Greek Literature and Belief*. Oxford: Oxford University Press.

Drachmann, A. B. 1912. *Diodors Römische Annalen bis 302 a. Chr. samt dem Ineditum Vaticanum*. Bonn.

Edelstein, Ludwig. 1967. *The Idea of Progress in Classical Antiquity*. Baltimore: Johns Hopkins Press.

Edmunds, Lowell. 1980. "Ancient Roman and Modern American Food: A Comparative Sketch of Two Semiological Systems." *The Comparative Civilizations Review* 5:52–69.

Ferrua, Antonio. 1964. "Nuove *tabulae lusoriae* inscritte." *Epigraphica* 26:3–44.

Flandrin, J. L., and Massimo Montanari, eds. 1999. *Food: A Culinary History*. New York: Columbia University Press.

Flensted-Jensen, Pernille, et al., eds. 2000. *Polis & Politics: Studies in Ancient Greek History. Presented to Mogens Herman Hansen on His Sixtieth Birthday, August 20, 2000*. Copenhagen: Museum Tusculanum Press.

Frederiksen, M. W. 1984. *Campania*. London: British School at Rome.

Friedländer, Ludwig. 1921–23. *Sittengeschichte Roms*. 10th ed. Leipzig: S. Hirzel.

Garnsey, Peter. 1988. *Famine and Food-Supply in the Greco-Roman World: Responses to Risk and Crisis*. Cambridge: Cambridge University Press.

Gourevitch, Danielle. 1974. "Le menu de l'homme libre, recherches sur l'alimentation et la digestion dans les oeuvres en prose de Sénèque le philosophe."

In *Mélanges de philosophie, de littérature et d'histoire ancienne offerts à Pierre Boyancé*. Rome: École française de Rome (Collection de l'Ecole française de Rome 22), 311–44.

Gowers, Emily. 1993. *The Loaded Table*. Oxford: Oxford University Press.

Horden, P., and Nicholas Purcell. 2000. *The Corrupting Sea, a Study in Mediterranean History*. Oxford: Blackwell.

Humm, Michel. 1997. "Les origines du pythagorisme romain: Problèmes historique et philosophique, l'origine tarentine du pythagorisme romain." *Les Etudes Classiques* 65:25–42.

Innes, D. C., H. M. Hine, and C. B. R. Pelling, eds. 1995. *Ethics and Rhetoric: Classical Studies for Donald Russell on His Seventy-Fifth Birthday*. Oxford: Oxford University Press.

Jacoby, Felix. 1949. *Atthis: The Local Chronicles of Ancient Athens*. Oxford: Oxford University Press.

Koortbojian, Michael. 2002. "A Painted *exemplum* at Rome's Temple of Liberty." *JRS* 92:33–61.

Leo, F. A. 1901. *Die griechisch-römische Biographie nach ihrer litterarischen Form*. Leipzig: Teubner.

Levick, B. M. 1982. "Morals, Politics and the Fall of the Roman Republic." *Greece and Rome* 29:53–62.

Lintott, Andrew. 1972. "Imperial Expansion and Moral Decline in the Republic." *Historia* 21:626–38.

Longo, Oddone, and Paolo Scarpi. 1989. *Homo edens: Regimi, miti e pratiche dell'alimentazione nella civiltà del Mediterraneo*. Milan: Diapress.

MacDonald, Marion, ed. 1994. *Gender, Drink, and Drugs*. Oxford/Providence: Berg.

Mele, Alfonso. 1981. "Il pitagorismo e le popolazioni anelleniche di Italia." *Annali del Istituto Orientale di Napoli, Archeologia e Storia Antica* 3:61–96.

Momigliano, Arnaldo. 1972. "Tradition and the Classical Historian." *History and Theory* 11:279–93. Reprinted as Momigliano 1977a, 161–77.

———. 1977a. *Essays in Ancient and Modern Historiography*. Oxford: Blackwell.

———. 1977b. "Athens in the Third Century B.C. and the Discovery of Rome in the Histories of Timaeus of Tauromenium." In Momigliano 1977a, 37–66 (first published 1959, *RSI* 71: 529–56).

Montanari, M. 1999. "Food Systems and Models of Civilization." In Flandrin and Montanari 1999, 69–78.

Nenci, Giuseppe. 1989. "Pratiche alimentari e forme di definizione e distinzione nella Grecia arcaica." In Longo and Scarpi 1989, 25–30.

———. 1999. "Il miglio e il panico nell'alimentazione delle popolazioni mediterranee." In Vera 1999, 25–35.

Paoli, U. E. 1963. *Rome: Its People, Life and Customs*. London: Longman, 1942. *Urbs, aspetti di vita romana antica*. Florence: F. Le Monnier, 1942.

Purcell, Nicholas. 1994. "Women and Wine in Ancient Rome." In MacDonald 1994, 191–208.

————. 1995. "On the Sacking of Carthage and Corinth." In Innes, Hine, and Pelling, 1995, 133–48.

————. 1996. "The Roman Garden as a Domestic Building." In *Roman Domestic Buildings*, ed. I. Barton. Exeter: Exeter University Press, 121–51.

————. 2003. "Becoming Historical: The Roman Case." In Braund and Gill 2003, 12–40.

Raaflaub, K. A. 2000. "Zeus Eleutherios, Dionysos the Liberator and the Athenian Tyrannicides. Anachronistic Uses of Fifth-Century Political Concepts." In *Polis & Politics: Studies in Ancient Greek History: Presented to Mogens Herman Hansen on His Sixtieth Birthday, August 20, 2000*, ed. Pernille Flensted-Jensen, et al., 249–75. Copenhagen.

Rawson, Elizabeth. 1969. *The Spartan Tradition in European Thought*. Oxford: Oxford University Press.

————. 1988. *Intellectual Life in the Late Roman Republic*. London: Duckworth.

Riposati, Benedetto. 1939. *M. Terentii Varronis De vita populi Romani libri IV ad Atticum, c. comm.*, Milan [2d ed. 1972].

Sancisi-Weerdenburg, Heleen. 1995. "Persian Food: Stereotypes and Political Identity." In *Food in Antiquity*, ed. M. J. Dobson, F. D. Harvey, and John Wilkins, 286–302. Exeter: Exeter University Press.

Scarpi, Paolo. 1989. "La rivoluzione dei cereali e del vino: Demeter, Dionysos, Athena." In Longo and Scarpi 1989, 57–66.

Silvestri, Domenico. 1999. "Per un progetto di indagine sulla terminologia alimentare nel mondo antico." In Vera 1999, 345–63.

Skutsch, Otto. 1985. *The Annals of Quintus Ennius*. Oxford: Oxford University Press.

Smethurst, S. E. 1952. "Cicero and Dicaearchus." *TAPA* 83:224–32.

Taylor, L. R. 1934. "Varro's *De Gente Populi Romani*." *CP* 29:221–29.

Too, Y. L. 2000. "The Walking Library: The Performance of Cultural Memories." In Braund and Wilkins 2000, 111–23.

Tusa Cutroni, Aldina. 1970. "I KAMPANOI ed i TURRENOI in Sicilia attraverso la documentazione numismatica." *KOKALOS* 16:250–67.

Vandermersch, Christian. 1994. *Vins et amphores de Grande Grèce et de Sicile IVe–IIIe s. av. J.-C.*, Naples: Centre J. Bérnard.

Vera, Domenico., ed. 1999. *Demografia, sistemi agrari, regimi alimentari nel mondo antico, Atti del Convegni Internazionale di Studi (Parma 17–19 ott. 1997)*. Bari: Edipuglia.

Webb, R. 2000. "Picturing the Past: Uses of Ekphrasis in the *Deipnosophistae* and Other Works of the Second Sophistic." In Braund and Wilkins 2000, 218–26.

Wehrli, F. 1944. *Dikaiarkhos* [2d ed. 1967]. Basel: B. Schwabe.

LAND AND SEA: ITALY AND THE MEDITERRANEAN IN THE ROMAN DISCOURSE OF DINING

JOHN WILKINS

Abstract. Discussions of dining in Roman literature often focus on moralising discourses of the satirists in the imperial period. This article seeks to extend the discussion in four areas: (1) a broader temporal frame, which runs from Cato the Elder to Athenaeus; (2) a wider cultural frame, which sets Greek commentaries of Rome alongside Rome's attitudes towards the Greeks; (3) a cultural range beyond Rome's elite, to the majority of the population; (4) a more ambitious literary frame, which presents Galen's discussion of food as texts of cultural richness rather than treatises reserved for medical historians.

ROMAN LITERATURE ABOUNDS with a rich series of dining scenes. Virro, the disagreeable Roman patron, entertains Trebius and other clients to a meal that is based on inequality, with the finest foods and tableware going to the host and the worst to Trebius. The meal is reciprocal, an exchange for services received, but a travesty of commensality. This is Juvenal's fifth *Satire*. There is Horace's bad host Nasidienus and his food-philosopher Catius (*Satires* 2.8 and 2.4). There is Petronius' creation, Trimalchio, the Greek freedman who is dripping with wealth and generosity but has no judgement for literature and no moderation at table (*Satyricon* 26–78). There is the sinister dinner of Domitian described by Cassius Dio (58.9), in which everything was black in order to terrify his Senatorial guests into thinking their last moment had come.[1] There are the outrageous meals of Roman governors in Cicero's speeches (*Against Verres* 2.3.68, 2.5.33), and in Seneca's letters there are comments on the lavish ceiling devices, saffron-pumping devices, and extraordinary appetites of the Roman elite (16.9, 90, 114.10, 122.5). At a more refined level, there are the meals revealed in the letters of Pliny the Younger (1.15, 2.6, 9.17, 9.36), in which different styles of food are provided for

---

[1] There are many points of contact between the private dining scenes and descriptions of dining with the emperor (both restrained and excessive), particularly in Suetonius' accounts of the reigns of Augustus and Caligula.

different classes of guest, and there is no shortage of entertainment. Pliny appears to understand his literature much better than does Trimalchio and is less cruel than Virro, but the social and intellectual activities are of the same kind.

Certain themes emerge very strongly. These include moral disapproval, a negative discourse that seeks to stem luxury and excess with excoriating ferocity. The negative discourses tend to focus on the evils of the marketplace (though Rome in the imperial period was one of the best centres of trade in the pre-modern period) and to praise the life of simple self-sufficiency. In this regard, we shall see Juvenal praising the products of his own farm and Trimalchio claiming to produce various exotica on his own estates.

The theme of dining intersects with many other discourses in Roman and Greek literature, particularly those which focus on luxury and excess. Certain themes in Seneca correspond to the approach that might be expected in Plato—simple foods, for example, are praised, the cook is rejected, as are all kinds of fancy embellishments of the home. I have discussed the discourse of luxury in Greek literature in chapter 5 of Wilkins (2000). The discourse is based on the fundamental human needs of shelter, food, and clothing. At a certain stage of development, a culture was considered to have developed excessive provision for these needs and to provide luxuries rather than essentials. Cooks are a striking example, for they offer a particularly high level of sophistication, whereas household slaves could supply nourishing food perfectly adequately.[2] The sophistication of the cook thus draws the attention of the moralist, as may be seen in Herodotus 9.82 (the tent of Mardonius), in Plato *Gorgias* 518, and in a number of Roman authors. A less moralising approach would consider cooks from the perspective of the court, the Persian court, the tyrant's court, the court of the Roman Emperor, and would consider such matters as its control of resources and its competition with others to display a certain level of cultural development (see Goody 1982, chap. 4; Hill and Wilkins 1993).

Gowers (1993) has demonstrated that, in Roman literature, food belonged to the less elevated genres, such as comedy, satire, and epigram. But dining is a much larger cultural phenomenon than literary genre alone. This article seeks to place Roman literary dining into a broader perspective that takes account of Rome's place in the Mediterranean world. The first section gives a temporal overview from Cato the Elder to

---

[2] On the servile status or otherwise of cooks, see Athenaeus 14.658e–62d; K. Latte, *Mageiros*, RE 14 (1930): 393–95.

Athenaeus. In the second section, dining is explored in relation to the food supply and patterns of eating outside the narrow concerns of the elite. The third section sets the dining literature in a further perspective, that of Galen, whose technical but rich cultural approach gives a strong contrast to the moralising discourses of Juvenal, Seneca, and Petronius.

A discussion of dining must take account of a number of features. For sophisticated dining, as opposed to surviving at a subsistence level, a surplus of food is necessary, such that those participating in the dinner are not eating merely to stay alive. Such dining is normally focussed on a court or other elite,[3] which has a claim to greater resources than others in the community. This elite can both demonstrate its superiority to outsiders by benefitting from the shared meal (more often seen in Greek than Roman culture) and distribute food and other benefits of the dinner in such a way as to demonstrate the social equality or inequality of the participants (more often seen in Roman than Greek culture). Such an elite is a likely stimulant to the employment of specialist cooks and the production of cookery books (Goody 1982).

In a broad Mediterranean context, we should note that the Romans developed distinctive styles of dining that were not unrelated to those of their neighbours, in particular the Etruscans to the north and the Greek cities of southern Italy. As far as food was concerned, there was a general movement west of foodstuffs. During the archaic period, the domestic fowl (still the "Persian bird" in Aristophanes) appears to have travelled much of its long journey from the forests of Thailand[4] to the Black Sea and thence into the Mediterranean world. Similarly, in earlier millennia, the technical knowledge for growing cultivated cereals, olives, and vines may have followed a westerly trajectory, though multiple local developments of cultivated forms of wild plants may also be a viable historical model. During Roman times, the peach and the apricot appear to have arrived successfully in the western Mediterranean, and Lucullus is said to have introduced the cherry into Italy. Was this action of Lucullus as problematic as other imports of luxuries from Asia Minor?[5] Galen, for his part, is ambivalent over the import of various eastern fruits. Wider concerns about empire have been grafted onto a cultural phenomenon that had been in process for some four millennia. This process was not confined to the foods of the dining table. The practice of reclining at dinner, and later of reclining in the formation of the triclinium, came to

[3] See Goody 1982.
[4] See Kiple and Ornelas 2000, I 496.
[5] On Lucullus, the cherry, and luxury, see Athenaeus 2.51a and 6.274e–f.

the Greek world from the Assyrians, apparently in the archaic period, and then on to Rome (see Roller, this volume). It was possible for Roman writers to place new practices and foods within the discourse of luxury, as their Greek predecessors had done, but, on other occasions, the new import might be accepted as part of a successful meal. So, to take an extreme example, Juvenal in the third Satire rails against the Syrian influence on Rome (the Tiber is said to be polluted by the Orontes), but in his idealised rustic meal in the eleventh *Satire*, he is happy to serve Syrian pears beside Italian apples, both apparently grown on his estate at Tivoli. Even the satirist does not wish to pretend that foods from pears to olives, from wheat to vines had not been introduced into Italy from the eastern Mediterranean. The pervasive influence on Roman literature of the tastes and smells of the foods of the Mediterranean world is explored at length in Dalby 2000.

Much of the negative discourse of dining clearly derives from complex concerns about empire and the extent to which Roman identity might be modified by the presence in Rome and Italy of other cultures, Syrian, Greek and many others. What is a concern for Juvenal is a theme for celebration in Aelius Aristides and Athenaeus, as we shall see shortly. Juvenal reinforces his claim for the rustic purity of Tivoli with the nostalgic Republican myth of M. Curius Dentatus, who raised green vegetables in his small garden and cooked them himself at his modest hearth. This charming scene, which diverts the minds of Roman readers from their slave-owning imperial mastery of the Mediterranean, evokes several centuries of Roman myth making in respect of dining.

A LITERARY COMMENTARY ON ROMAN DINING FROM CATO TO ATHENAEUS

Two pivotal figures in the mythography of dining are Cato the Elder and Ennius. Cato's celebrated opposition to Greek influence on Rome, and probably to Roman expansion in the Greek world, is epitomised in Polybius' report (31.25) that Cato took exception to the foreign luxuries that were being imported into Rome, namely, amphorae of salt fish from the Black Sea at 300 drachmae each and beautiful boys who cost more than land.[6] These objections went side by side with the somewhat contra-

---

[6] Polybius in this chapter endorses the view of Cato, noting that some of the Roman youth had abandoned itself to the love of boys and courtesans, to musical entertainments, and to banquets: "it was just at the period we are treating of that this present tendency to

dictory evidence of Cato's *De Agricultura*, which appears in parts to be constructed in the model of Greek predecessors, and in which there are elements that appear to derive from Greek influences. The recipe for ersatz Greek and Coan wine, if it was not possible to buy the original, implies a vogue for Greek wines in Italy. Cato's cakes have a number of Greek as well as Roman names, which again implies a demand for Greek foods and wines.[7] Even Cato had an ambiguous relationship with the Greek world as is clearly set out in Astin (1978), particularly in his eighth chapter, "Cato and the Greeks." Ennius, apparently the protégé of Cato, and a further recruit to the standard of Republican virtue, is nevertheless likely to have been educated in Greek and to have learnt Oscan and Latin. His native tongue was Messapic. It is no surprise, then, that he also wrote with Greek models in mind, and nowhere more so than in his hexameter poem the *Hedyphagetica*.[8] This appears to be an expanded Latin version of the *Hedypatheia* of Archestratus of Gela, which was written in the fourth century B.C.E. Ennius' version includes sites that were not known in the time of Archestratus (such as Clipea), and a number of Italian locations have probably been added to the original. It is not known whether Ennius included in his version the advice of Archestratus on how to dine (fr. 4 Olson and Sens, 2000): three to five people at one table. Eleven lines of the version of Ennius are quoted by Apuleius in his *Apologia* (39.2):

> Quintus Ennius wrote a *Hedyphagetica* in verse; he lists countless types of fish, which he has clearly studied carefully. I remember a few verses, which I will recite:
>
> Just as the sea-weasel[9] at Clipea surpasses all others,
> Mussels are most abundant at Ainos, rough-shelled oysters at Abydos.
> The scallop is found in Mytilene and in Ambracian Charadrus.
> The sargue is good in Brindisi; if it is big, buy it.
> Be aware that the boar-fish is of the highest quality at Tarentum.
> Be sure to buy the *elops* at Surrentum and the *glaukos* in Cumae.

---

extravagance declared itself, first of all because they thought that now after the fall of the Macedonian kingdom their universal dominion was undisputed, and next because after the riches of Macedonia had been transported to Rome there was a great display of wealth both in public and in private" (trans. Paton).

[7] On Cato's treatise, see further Astin 1978, 189–203; Dalby 1998.

[8] On the Greek influences on Ennius, see Jocelyn 1967, 12–27, and 1996.

[9] Probably the rockling, the *mustela marina*, to distinguish from the burbot, *mustela*, a river fish. See Andrews 1949.

Why have I passed over the parrot-wrasse, a veritable brain of Jove the
   Highest
(it is big and good when caught in Nestor's homeland),
the blacktail, the rainbow wrasse, the blackbird-fish, and the maigre?
At Corcyra there is octopus, fat bass heads,
Purple shellfish[10] large and small, mussels, and sweet sea-urchins.

He honoured many other fish with his verses, and (tells) among which
people, and how roasted or stewed, each of them tastes best.
                                                  (trans. Olson and Sens 2000)[11]

I have called upon two of the sternest figureheads of the Republic
to demonstrate that in the third and second centuries B.C.E., amidst the
debate on what the proper level of engagement in the Greek world
should be, Greek styles of dining (whether from the mainland or from
the Greek cities of southern Italy) remained a subject for attention in
Rome. This will come as no surprise to students of Gruen (1984) and
others who have charted the Hellenization of Rome from an early period; but it will come as a surprise to anyone who has read Roman dining
literature at face value.

Apuleius twice notes that Ennius had much advice on species of
fish and on the best methods for cooking them. This apparent favourable
treatment of the subject may be contrasted with Ovid's comment on fish
in *Fasti* 6 and Pliny's concerns in book nine of the *Natural History*. Of the
goddess Carna, Ovid writes (6.169–86):

You ask why fat bacon is eaten on these Calends, and why beans are mixed
with hot spelt.[12] She is a goddess of the olden time, and subsists upon the
foods to which she was inured before; no voluptuary is she to run after
foreign viands. Fish still swam unharmed by the people of that age, and
oysters were safe in their shells. Latium knew not the fowl that rich Ionia
supplies, nor the bird that delights in pygmy blood; and in the peacock
naught but the feathers pleased; nor had the earth before sent captured
beasts. The pig was prized, people feasted on slaughtered swine: and the
ground yielded only beans and hard spelt.   (trans. Frazer)

The ideology of Augustan Rome constructs republican Rome as an
agricultural community that is not influenced by the sea either in terms

---

[10] The murex or purple-shell.
[11] On these Latin verses, see the commentary of Olson and Sens 2000; Skutsch
1985, 3–4.
[12] The grain is probably emmer.

of the supply of fish or of imported foods. This construction is reinforced by the divine order. Similarly, Pliny the Elder remarks, after carefully listing various species of fish (9.53),

> why do I mention these trifles[13] when moral corruption and luxury spring from no other source in greater abundance than from the genus shell-fish? It is true that of the whole of nature the sea is most detrimental to the stomach in a multitude of ways, with its multitude of dishes and of appetiz-ing kinds of fish to which the profits made by those who catch them spell danger. (trans. Rackham)

Ennius appears to be writing in a different republican context from the moralising discourse on fish that pervaded the Greek and Roman traditions, as Davidson (1997) and Hordern and Purcell (2000) have demonstrated. Ennius is unlikely to have been unaware of those tradi-tions since the very title[14] of the poem of Archestratus advertises the dangers of its content. These dangers are frequently commented on in the contemporary comedies of Plautus and Terence, which identify Greek dining as at the very least a significant drain on family resources.[15] The poem of Archestratus is preserved solely by Athenaeus of Naucratis, a collector of rare and influential texts, who provides a valuable commen-tary on Roman as well as Greek literary dining.

Athenaeus, who, like Galen, was a Greek writing in the Roman Empire at the end of the second century C.E. with the aim of reviewing many centuries of written evidence on his topic, gives a further valuable perspective on the moralising discourse of Roman satire and philosophy. In the *Deipnosophistae*, Athenaeus is well aware of the concept of luxury, and indeed dedicates his twelfth book to the topic. The patron of the fictional feast, the Roman magistrate Larensis, makes a series of com-ments on Roman morality at various places in the book, for example on the invasion of Rome by luxury at the end of Book 6, and on the desirability of marriage (albeit in a Greek context) in the thirteenth book, which is on courtesans. In his survey of the Republic, Larensis

---

[13] The rhetorical formulation is noteworthy. Pliny's work rests on such "trifles" (*parva*).

[14] The poem was known in ancient libraries under several titles: see Athenaeus 1.4d–e: "Archestratus of Syracuse or Gela in the *Gastronomia*, as Chrysippus entitles it, or *Hedupatheia* according to Lynceus and Callimachus, or *Deipnologia* according to Clearchus or *Opsopoiia* according to others . . ."

[15] See the comic passages listed by Gruen 1984, 261, n. 63, to which add *Menaechmi* 127–225.

reports specifically, for example, on the restrictions on dining in the
Fannian Law of 161 B.C.E. (6.274c–e), on the increase of luxury deplored
by Cato (he quotes Polybius 31.25 on salt fish and beautiful boys), and on
the contribution to luxury of Lucullus during the Mithridatic Wars.[16] On
the subject of luxury, Athenaeus has more to add on one of the famous
gourmets known as Apicius (1.7a–b), some of whose cookery book may
have been transmitted to the late work now known as Apicius *De Re
Coquinaria*:

> there lived in the days of Tiberius a man named Apicius, an exceedingly
> rich voluptuary, from whom many kinds of cakes are called Apician. He
> had lavished countless sums on his belly in Minturnae, a city of Campania,
> and lived there eating mostly high-priced prawns [*karides*], which grow
> bigger there than the largest prawns of Smyrna or the lobsters of Alexan-
> dria. Now he learned that they also grew to excessive size in Libya, so he
> sailed forth without a day's delay, encountering very bad weather on the
> voyage. When he drew near those regions, fishermen sailed to meet him
> before he left his ship (for the report of his coming had spread far and wide
> among the Libyans), and brought to him their best prawns. On seeing them
> he asked if they had any that were larger, and on their answering that none
> grew larger than those they had brought, he bethought him of the prawns
> of Minturnae and told the pilot to sail back by the same route to Italy
> without so much as approaching the shore.   (trans. Gulick)

Athenaeus does not identify his source for this data (he may have
done, but the text depends solely upon the epitomator who stripped out
the bibliographical references), but he exemplifies the topos of the man
who seeks the best produce throughout the Mediterranean. It is a benefit
of empire that such an ambition should be possible, to acquire[17] the best-
known specimens from three continents; equally, we should note,
Archestratus and his translator Ennius provided just this information in
their gastronomic poems of the fourth and second centuries, respectively,
hundreds of years before the imperial period.

At the same time, Athenaeus embraces other approaches in addition to the theme of luxury. In the second book (50f–51b), he has Larensis

---

[16] We might add Athenaeus' quotation of Polybius Book 30 at 5.194c, in which
Antiochus Epiphanes competed with the Roman general Aemilius Paulus in providing
public feasts on the Greek mainland.

[17] Apicius seems to follow the model of Archestratus and Ennius, to go to the place
and be sure to buy the food, rather than Trimalchio and the Roman elite, who sought to
bring the best foods in the world to their own tables in Italy.

claim, "there are many things which you Greeks have appropriated as if you alone had given them names or were the first to discover them; but you are unaware that Lucullus, the Roman general who conquered Mithridates and Tigranes, was the first to import into Italy this tree from Cerasus, a city of Pontus. And he is the one who called the fruit *cerasus* ('cherry') from the name of the city, as our Roman historians record" (trans. Gulick). Larensis' claim is tellingly challenged, but the approach based on botanical terms removes the enquiry from the discourse of luxury that I noted above. Now the guiding principle is the system of classification and order in describing the natural world. We may compare Pliny 9.53, which is quoted above, for the statement that terminology and classification are "trifles" (*parva*) when compared with the overriding discourse of luxury.[18] A further approach embedded in Athenaeus is a primitive ethnography, which is best exemplified in the fourth book. On the dining customs of the Romans (in a survey of many peoples of the Mediterranean), Athenaeus quotes from the 110th book of the *Histories* of Nicolaus of Damascus:

> "the Romans staged spectacles of fighting gladiators not merely at their festivals and in their theatres, borrowing the custom from the Etruscans, but also at their banquets. At any rate, it often happened that some would invite their friends to dinner, not merely for other entertainment, but that they might witness two or three pairs of contestants in gladiatorial combat; on these occasions, when sated with dining and drink, they called in the gladiators. No sooner did one have his throat cut than the masters applauded with delight at this feat. And there have even been instances when a man has provided in his will that his most beautiful wives, acquired by purchase, should engage in duels; still another has directed that young boys, his favourites, should do the same. But the provision was in fact disregarded, for the people would not tolerate this outrage, but declared the will void."   (trans. Gulick)

This account, probably made more racy by Gulick's translation of *gunaikes* as "wives" rather than "women" has all the hallmarks of the outsider's view, which draws attention to a bloodthirsty foreign practice, offers a particular extreme case of it, but fails fully to come to grips with the cultural and social context. An Etruscan from within the culture might have described such activities quite differently. That said, it is worth reading Nicolaus with Suetonius' account of the public and private dining of the emperor Caligula.

---

[18] Fortunately Pliny devotes much space to such "*parva.*"

If Athenaeus can bring some ethnographical and historical background to the conduct of an apparently insane emperor, he can assist,
too, with the interpretation of parts of the *cena Trimalchionis*. Petronius
has his vulgar host serve a long series of pork dishes in fantastical forms,
with a good deal of entertainment in addition, from acrobats to the
recitation of Homer. Literary antecedents can be found for some of the
dishes such as Alexis' comic version of the astrological dish, which is
quoted by Athenaeus (2.60a–b),[19] and for some of the entertainments.
Athenaeus himself has much to say on the reception of Homer and Plato
in the Roman and Hellenistic periods. But more striking is Athenaeus'
citation of a rare literary item, a letter in a series exchanged between
Lynceus of Samos and a Macedonian known as Hippolochus in the late
fourth century B.C.E. Athenaeus notes the rarity of the document (4.128c),
and we may be reasonably confident that for this reason it was not
known to Petronius. In other words, this is evidence for cultural practice
in Macedonia that was imitated in Rome rather than a direct literary
source.[20] The letter of Hippolochus describes the wedding feast of Caranus,
to which twenty men were invited. They were given gifts to take away (as
are Trimalchio's guests at various stages in the meal), including Corinthian
bronze (which is a centrepiece on the dining table of Trimalchio). There
is a similar variety of meat at the feasts of Caranus and Trimalchio, and
meat dishes are similarly served on silver plates.[21] Both meals have little
emphasis on fish. The centrepiece of the meal is a roasted pig that is
stuffed with thrushes, ducks, warblers, and other foods, a more theatrical
version of which is described by Petronius in chapter 40. Both Trimalchio
and Caranus have mechanical devices to reveal surprises to the guests.
The entertainers at the Macedonian wedding include ithyphallic dancers,
clowns, and female acrobats, who breathed fire and tumbled among
swords while naked; Trimalchio's entertainers are acrobats, musicians,
and literary performers of various categories.

Thus we see that Petronius' colourful creation, Trimalchio, who
with his fellow diners probably exemplifies many characteristics of Greek
freedmen in Rome and Campania in the first century B.C.E. and may well
be in some respects a caricature of Nero or others at the imperial court,

[19] On this dish, see further Arnott 1996, 732–37.
[20] See note 6 for Polybius' comments on the Macedonian influence on Rome in the
second century B.C.E.
[21] See Dalby 1998, who, in discussing the feast of Caranus, notes that the combination of egg yokes and sow's womb appears in the meal of the Deipnosophists at 9.376c–d.
He believes Athenaeus, too, has followed this Macedonian lead.

nevertheless also recalls at table the kind of Macedonian and thence Hellenistic feast that Polybius and others had commented upon with alarm some three centuries earlier. If Rome was in the first century C.E. the imperial power for the peoples of the Mediterranean and beyond, was it necessary that upper-class dining be conducted in this mode (albeit without the satirical overlay)? The answer is clearly not, for Suetonius provides two models of dining for Augustus, one simple and austere and reminiscent of republican nostalgia, the other socially based and strongly hierarchical in the Roman manner.

A thenaeus supplies a further model. Larensis, the host of the learned Deipnosophistae, provides a series of courses at meals in his home, which has the best library in the world. The guests are served a great variety of foods—vegetables, fruits, breads, fish, meat, and so on—and are obliged to reveal their researches in the library before they can proceed to eat anything. The *Deipnosophistae* is thus a literary feast set at a banquet where everything is described, identified, and located in a text, but very little is eaten. This is the ultimate literary lunch. The majority of the diners are Greek rather than Roman, and they are clients of the great Roman host, as Whitmarsh (2000) has demonstrated. They bring their tribute of Greek literature to the new cultural centre of the world and constitute a new literary model in which Rome is not obliged to be the imperial city under siege from Greek culture but can claim to be the centre (the "ouranopolis," 1.20c) to which all the literature and all the food of the eastern Mediterranean is brought. This is close to the model proclaimed by Aelius Aristides in his fortieth oration.

DINING OUTSIDE THE ELITE

Much of the literature of dining produced by Roman culture concerns only the elite. Even where satirists such as Horace, Juvenal, and Petronius contrast the rich adversely with poorer citizens, their focus is on the deficiencies of Nasidienus, Virro, or Trimalchio. Poorer clients might be included at the feast but only to see the social chasm between them and their patron more starkly delineated than ever. The literary products of the elite also idealise the countryside, as we have seen, and so Juvenal's farm at Tivoli, Horace's in Sabine territory, Simylus' farm in [Vergil's] *Moretum,* and Dio Chrysostom's virtuous peasants in the *Euboean Oration* all highlight the moral purity of rural people, rather as Plato does in the *Republic*. There is no acknowledgement of the relentless toil that is necessary for the countryman to bring in from the farm enough food to

maintain his family through the Mediterranean year, or for the personal
and demographic costs explored by Garnsey (1999, 43–68). Garnsey has
said of malnutrition (60–61):

> Certain broad social divisions are very relevant to our subject [malnutri-
> tion], as reflecting a combination of environmental conditions and social/
> cultural customs and attitudes—such as, the different situations of men
> and women, and of city and country residents. One can predict that malnu-
> trition and morbidity would have been more widespread and more serious
> among women, especially those of child-bearing age, than among men, and
> among inhabitants of large urban agglomerations than among rural popu-
> lations. And one would expect to find, as in developing countries today,
> that malnutrition was predominately an affliction of children.

The dining literature of Rome portrays overwhelmingly adult male
diners[22] (the gender and age-range most likely to survive in the competition for food) and most often diners who benefit from the redistribution
of food through the client/patron relationship, whether a rich citizen to
his *clientela* or an emperor or benefactor to needy subjects and citizens.
Thus the autarchic[23] rural ideal favoured by Plato through to Juvenal is a
wistful rejection of the city as the best centre of exchange for food
supplies, just as the rejection of all the imported foods of empire that are
to be found in the international marketplace of Rome is a moralist's take
on a system of supply that is working very successfully for the imperial
metropolis.

It is important to note, however, that formal dining was not confined either to the ancient elites or exclusively to men, and that a very
different picture of ancient Italian and Mediterranean society would
have emerged if the texts had not chosen to concentrate on the urban
elites. We might then have seen dining at marriage feasts, at civic festivals, and at other gatherings that were not exclusive to men and were
certainly not exclusive to the ruling classes. It is notable that many of the
dining texts under consideration are set in private and secular venues,

[22] There are female diners, for example, at dinners in Petronius, Suetonius, and Ovid,
but such dinners are dominated by men. Women were often in control of household stores,
as they were in Athens, but that did not necessarily protect them from cultural norms that
favoured the males.

[23] The best satirical spoof on the theme of autarchy is Petronius *Cena Trimalchionis*
38, in which the host claims to produce mastic (*laina*: see Smith's commentary), cedar oil
(the text is disputed), pepper, Attic honey and Indian mushrooms on his own estates. See
above on Juvenal's production of Syrian pears.

which may be contrasted with those hallowed by tradition or religious ritual (a contrast exploited by Ovid in the *Fasti* passage quoted above). Such a contrast is a strongly ideological construction: when Galen comments on social occasions at which wine may be drunk, for example, he specifies (*On the Thinning Diet*), "at a drinking party, at a wedding, at a religious festival, or indeed at any other kind of celebration" (trans. Singer).

GALEN'S TECHNICAL TREATISES ON FOOD

Galen wrote a number of works on diet, exercise, bathing, and other aspects of life where doctors particularly expected to be able to monitor and improve the good health of their patients.[24] The advantages of Galen's approach are that it is distinct from the moralising discourse of the dining literature and can provide a commentary on it, that it has an overview that embraces all classes, and that he attempts to look at the picture over a long period, as does Athenaeus. He is thus another writer of the second century C.E. who is writing both for the present—as a practicing doctor—and in a review over many centuries back to Hippocrates in the medical libraries of the Hellenistic world. The doctor is much less exercised by fish than the moralising authors. Fish are simply a resource to be considered alongside other animal products. The doctor, too, gives much space (two-thirds of a long treatise) to cereals of all kinds (not only wheat and barley) and to fruit and vegetables: these products serve less well the ideological case but in fact represent what the majority of the population ate most of the time. Galen thus comments on the inadequacy of the diet at certain times of year, the spring in particular, for certain sections of the population—women and children in particular. He notes unsuitable parts of the diet that peasants tolerate because they have no choice, and he remarks that they send their best grain to the cities and eat inferior cereals themselves in order to balance better income against their own dietary needs. A number of Galen's illustrations come from incidents during journeys in Asia Minor, and his evidence is thus both medical from a scientific point of view and tested in the field. There is not any idealising of the countryside in these texts even though the author was physician to more than one emperor.

Galen and Athenaeus can be used to interrogate the well-known

---

[24] The main treatises in this area are *On the Powers of Foods*, *On the Thinning Diet*, *Hygieina*, and *On Simple Medicines*.

dining texts with which I began. I have already noted that the dinner of
Trimalchio appears to be modelled to some degree on Macedonian styles
of eating. It is clear that both Caranus and Trimalchio provide a large
amount of pork. We might suppose that Trimalchio does so because as a
former slave he wishes to provide large quantities of the most readily
available meat in order to impress his lower-class friends. He certainly
shows little interest in the imported birds or fish that appear in the text
of Apicius and are dismissed in the passage of the *Fasti* quoted above.
But pork might invoke the traditions of commensality whose passing
Juvenal laments in *Satire* 1:

> what a grossly ravening maw
> That man must have who dines off whole roast boar—a beast
> Ordained for convivial feasting!   (trans. Green)

Trimalchio and Caranus may both invoke the hunting traditions of ancient aristocracies. Galen's view is that pork is the best form of meat,
providing strength and also greater versatility than beef, which might be
damaging to some temperaments. Fish is found in the fourth *Satire* of
Juvenal as the great gift for the emperor, and in the fifth, in which the
meals of Virro and Trebius are contrasted:

> My lord will have his mullet, imported from Corsica or from
> The rocks below Taormina: home waters are all fished out
> To fill such ravening maws, our local breeding grounds
> Are trawled without cease, the market never lets up—
> We kill off the fry now, close seasons go by the board.
> Today we import from abroad for domestic consumption: these
> Are the luxury fish which legacy-hunters purchase,
> And which their spinster quarries sell back to the retailer.
> Virro is served a lamprey:[25] no finer specimen
> Ever came from Sicilian waters. When the south wind lies low
> Drying damp wings in his cell, then hardy fishermen
> Will dare the wrath of the Straits. But what's in store for you?
> An eel, perhaps (though it looks like a water-snake), or
> A grey-mottled river-pike, born and bred in the Tiber,
> Bloated with sewage,[26] a regular visitor to
> The cesspools underlying the slums of the Subura.   (trans. Green)

---

[25] In fact, a murry or moray eel.
[26] On the discourse of the Cloaca, see Gowers 1995.

Juvenal has added a number of ingredients to his main structure of the inequities of the client/patron relationship. His comments on the places to find the highest-priced fish, the premium paid for imports, and the implication of gluttony are all echoed in the verses of Archestratus and the commentary on them that Athenaeus employs when introducing the quotations (6.224b–c). The difference between eating a river fish and a sea fish, meanwhile, is commented on by Galen, as is, at some length, the pollution of the Tiber on which he writes (3.29):

> it is important to bear in mind with all fish the following common denomi-
> nator: that the worst fish are nurtured at the mouths of every river that
> flushes toilets, kitchens, baths, the dirt of clothes and linen, and everything
> else that is to do with the city that they run through which must be washed
> away, and especially when the city is densely populated. The flesh of the
> murry that lives in such water is found to be extremely bad, although it is
> impossible to find it either entering rivers or breeding in lakes. But never-
> theless the very worst is found at the mouths of these rivers, like the one
> that flows through Rome, which is why this fish alone is the cheapest of all
> those from the sea that are sold in this city, on a par with the fish that breed
> in the river itself.   (trans. Grant)

On the general moral objection to imported foods, Galen has no comment beyond the quality of the food. Thus capers are imported from Cyprus and have some beneficial properties, whereas carobs are difficult to digest, do not pass through the body quickly, are furnished with vari-ous bad qualities, and "it would be better if these fruits were not ex-ported from the areas in the east where they are grown" (2.33, trans. Grant). But he does comment on technical features, and river fish are not as good for the body as deep-sea fish, while river pollution is bad for all fish. And the pollution derives in part from those kitchens (*mageireia*) that so alarmed the moralists (or at least their denizens, the cooks, alarmed them).

CONCLUSION

The dining literature of Rome has an internal logic of its own, which is linked to the ideology of the early imperial period and is closely associ-ated with the imagined simple agricultural base of Republican politics that was quite distinct from the Hellenic influences on Italy. Similarly, the texts are concerned with the international commercial and social impact of empire and the effect these international pressures might have on the

Republican identity that the literary authors had constructed, particularly within the constrictions of the Roman client/patron system. A number of these concerns were in fact shared by Greek predecessors such as
Plato and were not wholly endorsed even by such Republican icons as
Cato the Elder and Ennius. A valuable overview to this body of texts is
provided by the Greek writers of the second century, Athenaeus of
Naucratis and Galen of Pergamon, both of whom engaged with eating
and dining in the Greek and Roman worlds but from a perspective that
was much broader than the dining literature.[27]

UNIVERSITY OF EXETER
e-mail: J.M.Wilkins@exeter.ac.uk

BIBLIOGRAPHY

Andrews, A. C. 1949. "The Codfishes of the Greeks and Romans." *Journal of the
    Washington Academy of Sciences* 39:1–20.
Arnott, W. Geoffrey. 1996. *Alexis: The Fragments, A Commentary.* Cambridge:
    Cambridge University Press.
Astin, Alan E. 1978. *Cato the Censor.* Oxford: Oxford University Press.
Braund, David C., and John M. Wilkins, eds. 2000. *Athenaeus and His World.*
    Exeter: University of Exeter Press.
Dalby, Andrew. 1988. "The Wedding Feast of Caranus the Macedonian." *PPC*
    29:37–45.
———. 1998. *Cato: On Farming.* Totnes: Prospect Books.
———. 2000. *Empire of Pleasures: Luxury and Indulgence in the Roman World.*
    London: Routledge.
Davidson, James. 1997. *Courtesans and Fishcakes: The Consuming Passions of
    Classical Athens.* London: HarperCollins.
Frazer, James G. 1929. *Ovid: Fasti.* London: MacMillan.
Garnsey, Peter. 1999. *Food and Society in Classical Antiquity.* Cambridge: Cam-
    bridge University Press.
Goody, Jack. 1982. *Cooking, Cuisine, and Class: A Study in Comparative Sociol-
    ogy.* Cambridge: Cambridge University Press.
Gowers, Emily. 1993. *The Loaded Table: Representations of Food in Roman
    Literature.* Oxford: Oxford University Press.
———. 1995. "The Anatomy of Rome from Capitol to Cloaca." *Journal of Ro-
    man Studies* 85:22–32.
Grant, Mark, trans. 2000. *Galen on Food and Diet.* With notes. London: Routledge.

[27] I am grateful to my reader from the Journal for suggesting a number of improve-
ments to this article.

Green, Peter. 1967. *Juvenal: The Sixteen Satires*. Harmondsworth: Penguin.

Gruen, Erich S. 1984. *The Hellenistic World and the Coming of Rome*. Berkeley and Los Angeles: University of California Press.

Gulick, Charles B. 1927–41. *Athenaeus: The Deipnosophists*. 7 vols. London and Cambridge, Mass.: Heinemann and Harvard University Press.

Hill, Shaun, and John Wilkins. 1993. "Mithaikos and Other Greek Cooks." In *Cooks and Other People*, ed. Harlan Walker. Totnes: Prospect Books.

Hordern, Peregrine, and Nicholas Purcell. 2000. *The Corrupting Sea: A Study in Mediterranean History*. Oxford: Blackwell.

Jacob, Christian. 2000. "Athenaeus the Librarian." In Braund and Wilkins 2000, 85–110.

Jocelyn, H. D. 1967. *The Tragedies of Ennius: The Fragments*. Cambridge: Cambridge University Press.

———. 1996. "Ennius, Quintus." In *The Oxford Classical Dictionary*, 3d ed., ed. Simon Hornblower and A. Spawforth. Oxford: Oxford University Press.

Kiple, Kenneth F. and Kriemhild C. Ornelas. 2000. *Cambridge World History of Food*. 2 vols. Cambridge: Cambridge University Press.

Olson, S. Douglas, and Alexander Sens. 2000. *Archestratos of Gela: Greek Culture and Cuisine in the Fourth Century B.C.* Oxford: Oxford University Press.

Paton, W. R. 1922–27. *Polybius: Histories*. London and Cambridge, Mass.: Heinemann and Harvard University Press.

Rackham, H. 1983. *Pliny: Natural History*. Vol. 3. London and Cambridge, Mass.: Heinemann and Harvard University Press.

Singer, Peter N. 1997. *Galen: Selected Works*. Oxford: Oxford University Press.

Skutsch, Otto. 1985. *The Annals of Q. Ennius*. Oxford: Oxford University Press.

Smith, Martin S. 1975. *Petronii Arbitri Cena Trimalchionis*. Oxford: Oxford University Press.

Whitmarsh, Timothy J. G. 2000. "The Politics and Poetics of Parasitism: Athenaeus on Parasites and Flatterers." In Braund and Wilkins 2000, 304–15.

Wilkins, John. 2000. *The Boastful Chef: The Discourse of Food in Ancient Greek Comedy*. Oxford: Oxford University Press.

HORIZONTAL WOMEN: POSTURE AND SEX
IN THE ROMAN *CONVIVIUM*

MATTHEW ROLLER

Abstract. This paper examines literary and visual evidence for women's dining posture at Rome. I distinguish actual social practice from the ideology of representation, while recognizing their interdependence. Contrary to the view that "respectable" women dined seated until the Augustan era, I argue that a women (of any status) could always dine reclining alongside a man, and that this signifies a licit sexual connection. The sitting posture, seen mostly in sub-elite visual representations, introduces further complexities of practice and ideology. In general, postures attributed to women function more as indicators of sexual *mores* than as direct representations of social practice.

I. INTRODUCTION

WHY, WONDERS ISIDORE, DID THE ROMANS refer to positions on the dining couches as *sedes*, when in fact they dined reclining? In answer he offers an historical explanation for which he invokes the authority of Varro. He writes, "*Sedes* are so-called because among the old Romans there was no practice of reclining, for which reason they were also said to 'take a seat.' Afterwards, as Varro says in his work *On the life of the Roman people*, men began to recline and women sat, because the reclining posture was deemed shameful in a woman."[1] Two generations after Varro, Valerius Maximus offers much the same information about ancestral convivial posture. Among the nuggets of information he provides "on old Roman customs" (*de institutis antiquis*), he writes, "Women ordinarily dined sitting next to men who reclined, a custom that passed from human dining practice to the gods: for at the feast of Jupiter, the

---

[1] Isid. *Etym.* 20.11.9: "sedes dictae quoniam apud veteres Romanos non erat usus adcumbendi, unde et considere dicebantur. postea, ut ait Varro de Vita populi Romani, viri discumbere coeperunt, mulieres sedere, quia turpis visus est in muliere adcubitus."

Illustrations appear in a gallery following page 114

49

god himself was treated to dinner on a couch, while Juno and Minerva sat in chairs." Valerius then dryly contrasts this longstanding divine dining practice to that of his own, mortal contemporaries: "Our own age cultivates this type of discipline more assiduously on the Capitol than in our own homes, evidently because it is of greater consequence to the state to ensure the orderly conduct of goddesses than of women."[2] By declaring that the seated convivial posture constitutes "orderly conduct" for a woman, and by noting that in his own day such conduct was no longer preserved "in our own homes," Valerius clearly implies two things: first, that by his day women were likely to be found reclining in *convivia* (the seated posture being retained only among the female gods at the *epulum Iovis*); and second, that this postural shift marks a moral decline. Likewise Varro, as quoted by Isidore, affirms that women's convivial posture was thought to have moral implications. The "old Romans," he says, regarded the reclining convivial posture as "shameful" in a woman, wherefore women dined seated. Varro also, like Valerius, probably implies a contrast with contemporary practice. For the fact that he bothers to explain an ancient practice together with its ethical underpinnings seems to imply that, in his own day, the practice is disused and its rationale generally forgotten.

These two passages are rich in implications about the ethical and social stakes of dining posture, especially that of women in contrast to men. On the one hand, these passages seem to make a concrete historical claim: that in an (undefined) early period, Roman women sat to dine while men reclined, whereas "now"—for the contemporaries of Varro and Valerius, each in his present moment—women, too, recline to dine, just as men do; they therefore must have changed their convivial posture at some point. On the other hand, these passages also make clear that the distinction between these two dining postures is ideologically fraught, especially along gendered lines—for they link the alleged shift in women's posture to overall moral decline.

Now, of these two aspects, the historical and the ideological, scholars to date have found the former most engaging. Indeed, there is a

<hr/>

[2] Val. Max. 2.1.2: "feminae cum viris cubantibus sedentes cenitabant, quae consuetudo ex hominum convictu ad divina penetravit: nam Iovis epulo ipse in lectulum, Iuno et Minerva in sellas ad cenam invitabantur. quod genus severitatis aetas nostra diligentius in Capitolio quam in suis domibus conservat, videlicet quia magis ad rem <p.> pertinet dearum quam mulierum disciplinam contineri." The *epulum Iovis* was celebrated twice per year, September 13 and November 13; hence Valerius can speak of it as a contemporary, observable phenomenon that, he supposes, preserves and transmits an archaic social practice.

scholarly *communis opinio* regarding what happened when. The accepted and widely disseminated view—enshrined in the authoritative handbooks of Roman social practice—is that, while men dined reclining, married women dined seated in *convivia* (prostitutes being another matter) through the bulk of the republican period. However, even these "respectable" women began to adopt the reclining posture by the last years of the republic, or perhaps in the Augustan period or early empire.[3] The ideological aspect, on the other hand, has only recently attracted any attention. Keith Bradley, in a recent article on familial dining practices (1998, 47), suggests that the seated posture functioned pragmatically, placing women under male scrutiny and control. Moreover he asserts that, whatever the vagaries of actual social practice, the seated posture for women remained at *all* times the "strict protocol," even in the imperial period. Thus Bradley not only understands women's convivial posture in the context of gendered social dynamics and social control broadly, but he employs this understanding to nuance the historical claim—for he makes the vital point that social values and social practice may not coincide neatly.

In this article I explore anew both the historical and the ideological questions just defined. For as Bradley intimates, they cannot be separated but must be considered together. We shall see, indeed, that any representation of women's dining posture is ideologically invested. Virtually no such representation in any medium, at any time or place, or among persons of any social status, provides direct, unmediated evidence for actual social practice. On the other hand, once we grasp the symbolic dimensions of women's convivial posture—its implicatedness with Roman sociosexual norms and values more broadly—we can also draw some conclusions about the social practices that were possible or probable at different periods and for persons of different statuses. The practical and ideological dimensions of dining posture thus refer to, presuppose, and symbiotically require one another. To open this discussion (section II), I survey the practice and ideology of convivial posture for

---

[3] This account is first articulated, to my knowledge, in Marquardt-Mau 1886, 300–301, and is repeated a decade or so later in the relevant articles in Pauly-Wissowa (e.g., Ihm, "cena," *RE* 3 (1899): 63–67). It reappears largely unchanged in handbooks and surveys down to the present (e.g., Balsdon 1962, 272; Dentzer 1982, 432) and is duly accepted by historical, literary, and archaeological scholars, who suppose that a view so widely diffused in authoritative reference works is well-founded (e.g., Christenson 2000, 269–70 (*ad* Plaut. *Amph.* 804); Wardle 1994, 225 (*ad* Suet. *Cal.* 24.1); Kay 1985, 123 (*ad* Mart. 11.23); Richardson 1988, 397–98).

adult males, since women's practices are typically articulated with respect to those of men. I then turn to women, examining representations of female conviviality and posture in three different media: literary texts, funerary monuments from the city of Rome, and Campanian wall paintings (sections III–V, respectively). These media differ both in their chronological range and in the social strata within which the corresponding representations were produced and consumed. I discuss these complications as I take up each body of evidence in turn.

II. DINING MEN: POSTURE, LEISURE, AND PRIVILEGE

From the late third century B.C.E.—the earliest period for which we have contemporary evidence—through the high empire, free adult males are represented as reclining to dine in the normal course of events. In Rome, as in the other cultures of the ancient Mediterranean for which reclining dining is attested, this posture marked a greater degree of social privilege and autonomy than any other dining posture (i.e., sitting or standing).[4] Here I examine a particular kind of privilege that this posture entailed for free adult Roman males: namely, the privilege of leisure (*otium*) and the various pleasures and luxuries that *otium* may comprise. Literary texts expose most clearly the association of reclining dining with *otium*, but the link is also visible—with different social consequences—in the convivial iconography of certain funerary monuments from the city of Rome and in panel-paintings that decorated the walls of dining rooms in several Pompeian townhouses.

The literary texts examined below were produced largely by and for a Rome-oriented male elite and tend to articulate elite urban values, anxieties, and practices.[5] In such texts, conviviality is often categorized under the rubric of *otium* and implicitly or explicitly contrasted with the

---

[4] Dentzer 1982, 431–47, discusses the cultural trajectory of the *banquet couché* from the near east to Greece to Italy to Rome, along with the aristocratic associations of this practice in each culture; esp. 432 on the greater privilege and status accorded to reclining than to sitting.

[5] Plautus is the exception to this characterization. Whatever his own social origins (traditionally non-elite), his dramas—unlike those of his successor Terence—do not seem to privilege elite concerns and viewpoints, nor do they speak predominantly to the elites within his audience. Yet even in Plautus, as we shall see, conviviality is largely an elite (or elite-dominated) activity. See Habinek 1998, 45–59, for the argument that early Latin literature (including Terence, but not Plautus) functions at least in part to consolidate and acculturate the mid-republican aristocracy; also Gruen's (1992, 202–22) remarks on Terence.

various *negotia*—the occupations or duties—with which elite Roman males not only busied themselves much of the time, but also defined themselves *as* elite Roman males: their own private social and economic affairs, legal advocacy on behalf of their clients or friends, and discharging magistracies or other military and administrative posts associated with government.[6] More generally still, conviviality in these texts may symbolize or instantiate something "pleasant," in contrast to "unpleasant" alternatives. While this characterization of elite conviviality should occasion no surprise, it seems worthwhile to cite a handful of literary passages, scattered across various genres and periods, to illustrate these associations.[7]

To begin with the earliest Roman literature, several Plautine dramas (late third to early second century B.C.E.) contain convivial scenes in which high-status males dine and drink while reclining in one another's company and alongside courtesans. The *convivium* is thus a place where such males enjoy a nexus of pleasures: wine, food, companionship, and the prospect (at least) of sex.[8] These convivial pleasures persist in the late republic as well. Cicero, early in his treatise on the ideal orator (*De Or.* 1.27), contrasts such pleasures with more serious activities and concerns (i.e., *negotia*). He relates that, when he was a young man, the senior senator and orator Cotta regaled him with a story from Cotta's own youth. Cotta said that he himself had participated one day in a gloomy and difficult discussion with certain *éminences grises* regarding the condition of the state. Following this discussion, however, when the party

---

[6] By "elite" I mean any member of the senatorial-equestrian aristocracy of the city of Rome, along with municipal aristocrats of other towns—those who had the wealth, birth, and acculturation to compete for magistracies and participate in government (whether they actually did so or not). With Hopkins 1983, 44–45, 110–11, I take this group as a single social entity, one largely unified (from the first century B.C.E. if not earlier, at least in Italy) by economic interests, acculturation, and socialization, whatever its political rifts. By "sub-elite" I mean anyone else, though in this paper the term is applied only to individuals who are clearly far removed from elites on all three standards (birth, wealth, and acculturation)—for which see Weaver 1967, 4–5.

[7] A bibliography on Roman leisure is just beginning to emerge. See Toner 1995, 11–33 (and *passim*), for an overview of the sociological and semantic questions; much in Edwards 1993, 173–206, is also pertinent. Leach 1999 offers an excellent, culturally engaged study of one aspect of elite *otium*. Less useful for current purposes are André 1966 and André et al. 1996, 229–451, which focus almost exclusively on literary and intellectual pursuits.

[8] E.g., Plaut. *Asin.* 828–32; *Bacch.* 1188–206; *Most.* 308–47. See section III below for more on the status of the males who recline to dine in Plautine comedy and on the "Greekness" or "Romanness" of the practices so represented.

repaired to the dining couches, the host Crassus dispelled the prevailing
gloom with his humanity, urbanity, and pleasantness. Cotta contrasts
these moods as follows: "in the company of these men the day seemed to
have been spent in the senate-house, while the dinner party seemed to
have been spent at [a suburban villa in] Tusculum."[9] That is, the grave
affairs of state (*negotia*), which filled the day's conversation, stereotypically
occupied the *curia* at the political heart of the Roman republican forum,
while the pleasurable, cheerful fellowship of the evening *convivium*
(*otium*) better suited a country villa. Cicero himself, says Plutarch (*Cic.*
8.4), almost never reclined for dinner before sundown, pleading a bad
stomach and also his *ascholia* (i.e., *negotia*) as keeping him away. Julius
Caesar, a busy man, rather eccentrically combined business with pleasure: Plutarch remarks upon the fact that he regularly dealt with his
correspondence while reclining at dinner.[10]

Moving onward, Horace contrasts *otium* and *negotium*, though not
necessarily in these terms, in some of his dinner-invitation poems (e.g.,
Carm. 2.11, 3.8, 3.29), for he dangles before his addressee—in each case,
a magistrate busy with public affairs—the enticements of companionship, sex, and especially wine, requesting that he seize these pleasures
and yield for the evening his anxious cares on behalf of the state.[11]
Likewise, one declamation in the elder Seneca's collection (*Cont.* 9.2)
posits that a provincial governor executed a criminal in the midst of a
convivium at a prostitute's request. Many of the declaimers who handle
this theme explore the shocking collapse of the *otium*/*negotium* distinc-

[9] Cic. *De Or.* 1.27: "tantam in Crasso humanitatem fuisse ut, cum lauti accubuissent,
tolleretur omnis illa superioris tristitia sermonis; eaque esset in homine iucunditas et tantus
in iocando lepos ut dies inter eos curiae fuisse videretur, *convivium* Tusculani." See also *De
Or.* 1.31–33, where *otium* is distinguished from the activities associated with the *forum*,
subsellia, *rostra*, and *curia*; also, *Mur.* 74 and Var. *Sat. Men.* fr. 336–40 Astbury (= Gell.
13.11.3–5).

[10] Plut. *Caes.* 63.7. Plutarch further notes at *Mor.* 619D–F that the *locus consularis*,
the position of the guest of honor on the low end of the middle couch, is advantageously
located for conducting such business as may come to this high-ranking man's attention
during the *convivium*—though the remark that "nobody crowds him, nor are any of his
fellow diners crowded" by this man's retinue (619F) implicitly acknowledges the tension
entailed by transacting business in an environment notionally devoted to leisure and
pleasure.

[11] On *otium* and *negotium* in Horatian dinner-invitation poems, see La Penna 1995,
268–70, and Murray 1985, 45–48. More generally on drinking, drunkenness, and *otium*/
negotium, see D'Arms 1995, 305–8.

tion that this situation envisions. For judicial matters, such as punishing criminals, belong in the forum, not the dining room; they should be done by daylight, not at night, and so on.[12] The younger Seneca, in *Ep.* 71.21, contrasts "lying in a *convivium*" with "lying on the rack" (i.e., for torture). The former, he acknowledges, is pleasant while the latter is unpleasant, yet the two kinds of reclining are indifferent in regard to Stoic moral value. Finally, Martial (*Epig.* 14.135) gives voice to an outfit of dining-clothes (*cenatoria*), which primly defines its proper realm by contrast with "serious" business: "neither the forum nor going to bail are familiar to us: our job is to recline on embroidered couches."[13] These passages are purely illustrative, and by no means exhaustive; they merely show how elite Romans consistently slotted conviviality into the category of *otium* and regarded it as encompassing a variety of specific pleasures: wine, food, conversation, companionship, sex. They also show how such Romans distinguished conviviality broadly, and the reclining posture that symbolizes it, from activities they perceived as serious or mundane (i.e. *negotia*), or unpleasant.

The privileges and pleasures associated with reclining to dine are thrown into higher relief when compared with the convivial postures and roles assumed by slaves. For slaves were excluded, by their postures as well as actions, from the leisure and pleasure enjoyed by the reclining diners—even as they were omnipresent around the site of the meal, and by their presence and service made the reclining diners' leisure and pleasures possible.[14] Literary texts normally show slaves on their feet, and often in motion as well—bringing food, pouring wine, clearing the tables, and the like. The younger Seneca (*Ep.* 47.3) evokes the image of wretched, hungry slaves standing all evening in silence—any noise to be punished with a whipping—attending at an imperious master's meal. Likewise, toward the end of his dinner party, Petronius' Trimalchio (74.6–7) turns around on his couch to address slaves (apparently) standing behind, dismissing them from service so that they can eat. Shortly before

---

[12] E.g., Sen. *Cont.* 9.2.4 (Hispo), 9–10 (Capito), 14 (Montanus), 22 (Argentarius), 24 (Latro); esp. 27 (Murredius): "serviebat forum cubiculo, praetor meretrici, carcer convivio, dies nocti," where *negotium* is the category governing the first term in each pair, and *otium* governs the second.

[13] Mart. 14.135: "nec fora sunt nobis nec sunt vadimonia nota: / hoc opus est, pictis adcubuisse toris."

[14] In general on slaves in *convivia*, with abundant sources, see D'Arms 1991; also, Foss 1994, 53–56.

their dismissal, however (70.10–13), they crowd onto the couches and recline briefly among the guests, at their master's express invitation. This is apparently an equalizing gesture, directed by the host, himself a former slave, to those who now fill the kind of station he once filled. Similarly, Martial catalogues the actions of a troupe of slaves who stand and move about a dining room, attending to the most menial bodily needs of their master (*Epig.* 3.82.8–17), and Juvenal (5.64–65) describes a handsome cup-bearer who disdains to serve his master's guests, resenting that the guests recline while he himself stands. These texts, though satiric, all presuppose that standing and moving about is the norm for slaves in *convivia*, and that this posture along with the service it implies marks slaves off as socially inferior to the reclining, stationary diners. Slaves are instrumental to the leisure and various pleasures of those who recline, without (in normal circumstances) enjoying that leisure and pleasure themselves. Occasionally slaves do appear reclining or sitting in *convivia*, but only when they thereby especially enhance the atmosphere of plea-sure and *otium* for the privileged reclining diners—for example, when they are favorite children or sexual objects. More on this matter below.[15]

Many associations of the reclining posture found in literary texts are also articulated iconographically, though to different social effect. Consider first a grave altar from the city of Rome, dating to the early second century C.E. and now in the Capitoline Museum (fig. a; B 830). It must stand for a number of such monuments that cannot be discussed here (though two others are discussed in section IV below). A relief at the bottom of this altar shows a man reclining on a *lectus* that has high boards at the head and foot, which are curved in a gentle S-shape. It also has a high backboard, difficult to see in this image. This man is propped upon his left elbow so that his torso is upright; his right knee is elevated while his left leg rests upon the mattress. This bodily disposition I hence-forth call the "classic dining posture." His torso is bare, but a mantle covers his hips and legs. He holds a drinking vessel in his left hand and a crown in his right. In front of the couch, within the diner's reach, stands a small table with three curved legs, upon which rests several implements

---

[15] Thus the female slave-prostitutes in Plautine comedy recline with the elite males to whom they provide sex (*Asin.* 830–32; *Bacch.* 79–81, 139–42, etc.). Also, at Trimalchio's *convivium* (Petr. 68.4–8) a youthful slave recites Vergil while sitting on the foot of the couch where his master Habinnas reclines. This boy, as subsequent comments reveal, is his master's pet educational project (hence the recitation) and also the object of his sexual attentions. Such cases merely confirm that a slave's role in the *convivium* is instrumental: to enhance the pleasure of the privileged and reclining diners in any way required.

or items of food that are difficult to identify here (though easier on other monuments, as we will see). At either end of the couch stands a male figure in a short *tunica* girt at the waist, the one at the foot holding a vessel in his right hand; both are of smaller stature than the reclining man. Comparison with the literary representations discussed above— some of which are roughly contemporary with this altar—reveals that these standing figures are undoubtedly slaves, tending to the wants of the man reclining at leisure. Above this tableau, the inscription identifies the deceased as C. Calpurnius Beryllus, freedman of Gaius, age 21.[16] It seems reasonable to identify the free adult male who is named in the inscription with the reclining (hence privileged) adult male in the relief beneath the inscription. Thus, Beryllus is commemorated in the guise of a reclining diner attended by slaves.

This relief displays a number of features that we will see are typical of convivial iconography. First, a hierarchy of postures distinguishes the figures: the free adult male reclines at leisure and the slaves stand in service. Second, the reclining diner is surrounded by objects that are probably to be regarded as carrying high prestige, signaling a distinctively elite form of dining luxury and pleasure. One possible prestige object is the small three-legged table. Such tables, as we shall see, commonly appear in these scenes and are often depicted with elaborately carved zoomorphic legs and feet. The curved legs here may be an attempt to suggest legs of this sort. Literary sources further indicate that dining tables of various sorts—even the smallish, round, three-legged variety such as this one—could be made of precious materials and as such might contribute materially to the host's display of his status and wealth.[17] The couch, too, is perhaps to be thought of as a prestige object. One such *lectus*, having (like this one) high endboards and backboard, but decorated with an elaborately patterned inlay, is known from

[16] "D M / C Calpurnius / C lib Beryllus / hic situs est / vix ann XXI" (*CIL* VI 14150). In addition to Boschung 1987, 107, no. 830, and Taf. 42, see Altmann 1905, 152 and fig. 124; Jones 1912, 353–54, no. 14a and pl. 89 (who identifies the objects on the table as a dish and a spoon).

[17] For dining tables of rare and precious materials, especially tops made of exotic veined woods, see Hor. *Serm.* 2.8.10–11; Sen. *Tranq.* 1.7; *Ben.* 7.9.2; Plin. *Nat.* 13.91–102; Stat. *Silv.* 4.2.38–39; Mart. *Epig.* 12.66.7, 14.89–90; also Amedick 1991, 23. On the other hand, such tables are apparently very modest at Hor. *Serm.* 1.3.13 and Ov. *Met.* 8.660–63. Three-legged tables in prestigious materials like marble and bronze have been recovered archaeologically (Richter 1966, 111–12); even the wooden ones known from Herculaneum are at least made of hardwoods to accommodate the decorative carving (Mols 1999, 129). For the zoomorphic legs, see Mols 44–45.

Herculaneum.[18] More certainly prestige objects are the slaves themselves, who stand at attention to the left and right of the couch. Their very presence implies that the diner's household has a certain degree of wealth—enough, at any rate, to purchase and maintain at least a couple of domestic slaves. Moreover, these particular slaves, whose smaller stature suggests that they are adolescents and not yet adults, are probably to be imagined as notably beautiful, sexually desirable boys. For adolescent males of this description, as literary texts indicate, were among the most highly prized and expensive of slaves. In elite households they commonly served wine in *convivia* (note again the vessel held by the slave at the left); as such they were among the beautiful, expensive, luxurious accoutrements that the elite host exhibited in an effort to impress and delight his guests.[19] Their slightly bulky hairstyle—fairly common in the iconography of youthful male slaves—may also signal their sexual desirability, since such slaves are sometimes described in texts as "long-haired."[20] Indeed, our reclining male diner may enjoy the prospect of an imminent sexual encounter since the owner of such slaves could be expected to make sexual use of them immediately after the *convivium* or at any other time.[21] Thus, the privileged, reclining, free adult male represented in this scene is the focal point of a number of pleasures. He enjoys food

[18] For such couches from Herculaneum, see Mols 1999, 35–42, 124–27, and cat. nos. 1–13; cat. no. 13 has the inlay in question (figs. 87–93).

[19] For the sexual desirability and expense of adolescent male cupbearers (the Ganymede figure) in elite *convivia* of the late republic and early empire, see, e.g., Sen. *Ep.* 47.7, 95.23–24; Petr. 92.3–5 (downscale version); Mart. *Epig.* 1.58, 9.25, 10.98, 11.70, 12.66.8 (etc.); Juv. 5.56–63; Suet. *Caes.* 49; and D'Arms 1991, 175–76. Slaves not fitting this profile make for less-refined *convivia*: see Cic. *Pis.* 67; Juv. 5.52–55.

Other funerary monuments from the city of Rome likewise depict slaves whose proportions appear to be those of adolescents or smaller children (see below). In my view, these cannot be instances of "proportional scaling" as seen on (e.g.) Romano-German grave reliefs of the first century c.e., where adult slaves are represented at a much smaller scale than the central figures on the couch to indicate their lesser importance (see, e.g., Galsterer-Galsterer 1975, nos. 196, 219, 228). I have found no clear instances of such "proportional scaling" of slaves on funerary monuments from the city of Rome proper.

[20] These slaves' hair, though not "long" in the sense of reaching their shoulders or beyond, is also not closely cropped; it is comparable to the slave hair seen on two urns, S 458 and S 462 (much longer on the extraordinary altar B 852), though the slaves in these latter cases are younger. For such hair as an attribute of luxurious, sexually desirable slave boys, see the iconographic and literary evidence collected by Fless 1995, 56–63.

[21] For the master having sex with his handsome slave boys directly following the *convivium*, see Sen. *Ep.* 47.7, 95.24 (similar implication at Petr. 92.3–4, 94.1–6). On slaves of both sexes as sexual objects, see Williams 1999, 30–38; Bradley 1987, 116–18; Neraudau 1984, 353–62.

and wine, kept in good supply by valuable, high-prestige, sexually excit-ing slaves standing in attendance, and surrounded by what is perhaps to be understood as showy, expensive furniture. These are precisely the sorts of pleasures manifested in literary representations of leisured elite conviviality, as discussed above.

What could such an image mean? Why might a deceased freedman be commemorated in the guise of a diner, reclining amidst the trappings (or allusions to the trappings) of elite conviviality? To begin with, this scene probably does not "realistically" illustrate the way Beryllus actu-ally dined during his life. Undoubtedly he dined reclining, at least after gaining freedom and citizenship. But could he have afforded the luxuri-ous accoutrements—the valuable slaves, perhaps the furniture—that are depicted or alluded to iconographically? Assuredly, Beryllus, or whoever commemorated him, was not impoverished: grave altars are a substantial form of commemoration (though seldom used by the Roman elite). On the other hand, this particular monument is a smallish example of the form and not of outstanding workmanship.[22] Thus, the "realistic" details of luxurious, elite dining make a claim to wealth and status on behalf of the commemorand that other physical aspects of the monument do not support.[23] But "realism" is not the only clue to meaning. For instance, there is no evidence that Roman males ever actually dined with bare torsos wearing only hip-mantles, as Beryllus does here. On the contrary, in literary texts ranging from the mid first to early second centuries C.E.—the period of this monument—we hear of an ensemble of garments, the

[22] The preserved height of the ancient stone, from the base of the columns to the cornice above the capitals, is 59 cm; the base and crown are modern. Originally, the monument no doubt had a base and pediment, which would have increased its height an unknown amount (ca. 20 cm?). Even so, it is smaller than the average height of a funerary altar. An unscientific survey of the first fifty or so altars in Boschung's catalogue yields an average height of about 90 cm.

[23] While a large, elaborately decorated monument likely implies that the deceased (or at least the dedicator) was wealthy and probably of high social status, the reverse claim—that a relatively modest monument implies relatively modest social status—is more problematic. For example, the few known altars commemorating elites (e.g., B 1 and 287, Calpurnii Pisones) are large but austere, and based on their form and decoration alone might not be expected to belong to lofty, wealthy aristocrats. Yet an altar alone may or may not indicate the material level of the burial overall: it may, for instance, have sat originally in a richly decorated family tomb, as those of the Calpurnii likely did. Nevertheless, given the Romans' penchant for self-advertisement, it seems probable that smaller altars with poorer decoration *on average*, if not universally, reflect lower status and wealth than larger altars with richer decoration.

synthesis or *cenatoria* (whose exact appearance is unknown) that men
normally wore for dining, and several texts suggest that any exposure of
flesh in a convivial context is exceptional and transgressive.[24] The point
of this motif, however, is hardly to suggest that Beryllus is an outra-
geously rude diner. Rather, scholars compare this nudity (which, as we
shall see, is fairly common in dining scenes) with the nudity that often
costumes gods and heroes in Graeco-Roman iconography, and on this
basis they deem it a "heroizing" motif, a positive attribute, to be sure, and
one that also removes the reclining figure from the realm of the ordinary
and places him in a somewhat elevated sphere.[25] It follows that the nude
torso signals an *abstraction*: it divorces the image from any specific,
actual *convivium* and instead enlarges the image's frame of reference,
inviting viewers to think in general terms about the social values articulated by the image. Through idealizing abstraction, then, the specificity of
the particular instance is converted into the generality of the *exemplum*,
which aspires to transcend contingency and to embody a universal,
diachronically valid canon of socially valorized behaviors, ideals, and
values.[26]

This relief, then, shows Beryllus not (necessarily) as he actually
dined but as the central figure in a generalized, stereotyped scene of elite
dining, which ties him to the values and ideals associated with such
dining: *otium*, privilege, luxury, and various specific pleasures such as
wine, food, companionship, and sex. Romans across a range of social
classes could have regarded such dining, and its associated values, as
refined, cultured, and indeed characteristically Roman, precisely because
of its elite associations, since elites were the persons in society who most
quintessentially "belonged." The deceased, then, is commemorated as
having embraced such values himself, and he exemplifies them for any-

[24] For the *synthesis* as dining garb, see Mart. *Epig.* 5.79, 14.1.1; *CIL* VI 2068.8; on
cenatoria, see Petr. 21.5, 56.9; Mart. *Epig.* 10.87.12, 14.136; in general, see Schuppe, "synthesis," *RE* 4A (1932): 1459–61; Marquardt-Mau 1886, 570–71. For condemnations of convivial
nudity, see e.g. Cic. *Ver.* 2.3.24; *Cat.* 2.23; *Pis.* 22; *Deiot.* 26; Vell. Pat. 2.83.2. Heskel 1994, 136–
39, discusses the meanings and implications of the adjective *nudus* ("naked" or "improp-
erly dressed") in these Ciceronian passages.

[25] On "heroic" nudity in Roman statuary, see Zanker 1988, 5–8. For the nude torso in
dining scenes as a "heroizing" motif, see Amedick 1991, 13; Ghedini 1990, 38; Himmelmann
1973, 18. Such "heroization" need not imply that the dead is envisioned as existing in a
blessed afterlife (so Ghedini 1990, 45–48): the motif can merely mark an idealization or
abstraction, without implying any specific eschatology.

[26] For "unrealistic" elements in Roman art signaling an abstraction, see Koortbojian
1995, 29–30; Hölscher 1987, 50–54.

one who examines his monument. Moreover, the fact that a former slave is shown attended by slaves has particular point: the slaves call to mind the freedman's former, enslaved self, and, through the contrast in postures, this freedman starkly distinguishes the social condition he achieved from that in which he began (and they remain). The message for the viewer, then, is one of both social differentiation and social integration. On the one hand it says, "the deceased transcended his erstwhile slavish condition and achieved a position of privilege relative to others." On the other, it says, "the deceased was—or at any rate should be remembered as being—a refined, cultured, exemplary Roman citizen, a good thing to be." To slaves who viewed this monument, it suggested that freedom, autonomy, and social integration were achievable (or had been achieved by some). To freedmen and their descendents, themselves new or recent entrants into the ranks of Roman citizens, such iconography declared that persons like themselves had achieved social belonging—had embraced and immersed themselves in central Roman values and practices—through their appropriation of this key elite artifact, namely, a certain style of dining.[27]

Visual representations of men dining in luxurious, leisured settings also survive from an entirely different social context—namely, as mural decoration in Campanian townhouses. These images offer another perspective on the cultural meanings of reclining dining, one different from those offered by literary texts and funerary monuments. Here again, the analysis of a single painted scene in its domestic context will have to stand for a large number. Another such scene will be discussed in section V below.[28]

The scene in question is found in the recently excavated (and still incompletely published) Casa dei Casti Amanti in Pompeii (IX.12.6–8). A provisional plan, published early in the excavation, seems to indicate that one entered from the street into a central hall (perhaps not a canonical *atrium*) with which various rooms were associated. The structure contained a bakery, including a large oven, millstones, and stables for the horses or donkeys that turned them; a shop for selling the bread

[27] On how elite habits, objects, and values provide models for sub-elites who are striving to belong, see Wallace-Hadrill 1994, 169–74 (and chap. 7 *passim*); Dexheimer 2000, 82; D'Arms 1999, 311.

[28] Of the ca. 25 Campanian panel paintings of dining scenes of which I am aware, virtually all are of the late third to fourth Pompeian styles, with the latter period better represented than the former; most therefore date ca. 30–79 C.E. Thus they overlap chronologically with some of the funerary monuments and literary texts under discussion.

was also attached (at no. 7).[29] A room adjoining the central hall to the north and east measures approximately 4 x 8 meters and looks out onto a garden through a window in the south wall (the door is toward the south end of the room's west wall). The room is decorated with red and black panels of the late third style (30s–40s C.E.); the east, north, and west walls sport well-preserved central panel-paintings, all of which are convivial scenes. This room's size, dimensions, view-lines into the garden, and pattern of central panel decoration all suggest that it is a dining room, a *triclinium*—a space designed and decorated with a view to holding *convivia*, though its actual uses at various times may have been more diverse.[30] Apparently, then, this structure had both living and industrial or commercial functions, that is, its final occupant was presumably a baker—assuredly a sub-elite—who conducted his business out of this unit but also maintained a well-decorated dining room in which to entertain guests. These guests, to judge from patterns found in literary texts, are likely in most cases to be the host's social peers or inferiors, men as well as women (as we shall see in section III below).[31]

Here I discuss the panel on the west wall of this room, because in most respects it typifies other panel paintings with convivial scenes and also permits edifying comparison with the funerary relief just discussed.[32]

[29] Varone 1993a provides a detailed but preliminary publication of this structure. For the ground plan (as it was known in 1988), see 619–20 and 632 fig. CLII, 1. At that time, the structure was not yet known to contain a bakery. For a description of the finds and structures associated with baking, see Varone 1993b, 8–9.

[30] Varone 1993a, 622, explicitly identifies it as a *triclinium;* for discussion of this room and its paintings see 622–29 (with accompanying images). Recent years have witnessed much scholarly discussion and reevaluation of the traditional methods for identifying the functions of rooms in Campanian houses; however, I am persuaded that most criteria traditionally used to identify *triclinia* are sound. For recent discussion see Dickmann 1999, 215–19; Dunbabin 1996, 67–70 (and *passim*); Zaccaria Ruggiu 1995, 139–42 and 144–46 (and *passim*); Ling 1995, 240 (and *passim*); critical remarks in Allison 2001, 192–93.

[31] Literary texts overwhelmingly represent hosts as being of a status higher than or equal to their guests. For rare attestations of sub-elites inviting elites to dinner, see Cic. *Fam.* 7.9.3, 7.16.2; [Quint.] *Decl. Min.* 301. Situations where elites invite higher-ranking members of their own group to dinner—equestrians hosting senators, or any such person hosting an emperor (e.g., Hor. *Carm.* 2.11, 3.8, 3.29; *Serm.* 2.8; Sen. *Ira* 3.40; Plin. *Nat.* 14.56; Suet. *Tib.* 42.2; Plut. *Mor.* 759F–60A)—should perhaps be considered special cases of "hosts inviting their peers," on the view that the senatorial-equestrian aristocracy constituted a unified socioeconomic group; see n. 6 above.

[32] This painting is illustrated in Varone 1993a, 637 (color); Varone 1993b, 8 (black and white); and online at <www.archart.it/archart/italia/campania/pompei/pompei.htm>, image no. 14 under "chaste lovers." I could not obtain permission to reproduce this painting in time for this article's publication.

In this panel, two couches are arranged at approximately a right angle, each occupied by a male-female couple. The men have darker skin than the women, as they often (but not always) do in paintings. Both men have nude torsos and recline in the higher position on their respective couches (i.e., at the head), while the women recline below them (i.e., toward the foot). All four figures support themselves on their left elbows in postures that resemble, but are not quite, the "classic" dining posture defined above. Both women lean against their men's chests; both also clutch large drinking vessels. Near the head of each couch, in the foreground, stands a three-legged wooden table—the rightmost one having lion feet like the majority of such tables on the funerary monuments (e.g., fig. b below), while the other is hoofed. Both, moreover, bear a set of drinking vessels and ladles like the tables on many of the funerary monuments (see below). These implements appear to be silver, comprising an entirely respectable if not strikingly luxurious drinking service, conspicuously displayed.[33] A slave is present in the scene, marked off in the familiar way—by his standing posture—as a social inferior discharging an instrumental function. Specifically, he props up a woman who, though on her feet, seems on the verge of toppling over backward, rolling her eyes upward and clutching a drinking vessel in an unsteady manner. Aside from the slave, all of these figures wear wreaths on their heads, a common convivial motif. One further figure appears in the scene. On what is presumably a third couch between and behind the two visible ones, a man (as evidenced by the darker skin and close-cropped hair) lies flat on his back, his head in profile and his eyes closed; his right arm is folded behind his head and his elbow points upward. Thus this painting, though compositionally a two-couch arrangement, in fact depicts three, hence a *triclinium*, properly speaking.

This description has stressed the iconographic similarities between this scene and the Beryllus monument; however, these scenes also diverge significantly. First, the composition of the painted scene is more complex with multiple couches[34] and many human figures. Also, these

---

[33] A much grander silver service is depicted as lying out on display in a fresco from the tomb of Vestorius Priscus; see D'Arms 1999, 311, and Dunbabin 1993, 119, for black and white images. For an actual luxury silver drinking service—the hoard from the House of the Menander—see Painter 2001, 14–25.

[34] These couches also lack the backboards and endboards seen on the many of the funerary reliefs. The reason for this difference is obscure to me, unless the choice is purely compositional, that is, couches depicted with high boards would block the view of some of the figures and portions of the background in the painted scenes, while the funerary reliefs seldom have any depth of field to obscure.

figures' bodily dispositions are vastly more dynamic than that of Beryllus (or of the convivial figures on funerary monuments generally). Their dining postures are not *quite* the "classic" one. They turn their heads this way and that, and some recline more on their backs than on their sides. Three of the four gesture vigorously to the left side of the scene as if in lively conversation, perhaps discussing what should be done about the reeling woman. In short, the scene has a narrative character that is absent from the funerary relief, which seems merely to signify.[35] Second, the painted *convivium* takes place within a carefully delineated architectonic setting, a space whose decoration complements the respectable tableware, furniture, and the like. On the funerary monuments, in contrast, the convivial reliefs seldom have much depth. Sculptors do not seek to enhance the overall sense of convivial luxury by this means (see figs. a, b, c). Third, while texts describe the pleasures of convivial wine drinking, and while funerary monuments like Beryllus' allude to them, the painting puts them graphically on display. The woman (barely) standing at the left, whose drinking vessel suggests she is reeling from wine, probably belongs on the couch of the supine man in back, who himself has apparently passed out from drinking.[36] Likewise, the woman on the rightmost couch holds an overturned glass in her dangling arm, another motif suggesting intoxication. Finally, the men's bare torsos not only "idealize" the scene but also eroticize it, as the women recline against these torsos in intimate physical contact. Thus, on the one hand, the painting and the funerary monument share the same basic iconographical elements pointing to the leisure and luxury of reclining dining, as described in elite literary texts: notably, the pleasures of food, wine, companionship, conversation, and eroticism, all in surroundings ranging from comfortable to luxurious. They also share the "idealizing" motif of the nude torsos, and in addition the diners in the painted scene are all ideally youthful and beautiful. Accordingly, the painting, like the monument, announces that it depicts no actual, specific dining situation but rather a generalized scene of the pleasures of high-style conviviality, and seeks to foreground the values associated with it. On the other hand, the monument and the painting differ in that the former merely hints at or

---

[35] For this distinction, see Dentzer 1982, 18.

[36] For drunken diners supine, see the panel on the opposite wall of the same room (Varone 1993a, 640, discussion at 629; image no. 13 on the website cited in n. 32); also, Suetonius reports that the emperor Claudius regularly finished *convivia* supine and asleep on his couch from too much food and wine (*Cl.* 8, 33.1).

alludes to these elements, while the latter heightens and even exaggerates them by displaying the drunkenness and sexuality with special gusto.

Remarkably, three other Pompeian townhouses—all houses of substance, but not among the grandest—contain dining rooms decorated with such dining scenes. The social dynamics of all such rooms are probably similar. In them, prosperous but sub-elite proprietors host *convivia* for (mostly) their social equals and inferiors.[37] What such hosts and their guests may have made of such paintings, viewing them as they themselves reclined to dine in these very rooms, I discuss in section V below. For to grasp the range of meanings these viewers may have found in such scenes, we must next examine the practice and ideology of women's convivial posture, the principal topic of this paper. Since central aspects of women's conviviality are often articulated, implicitly or explicitly, with respect to men's conviviality, and since we have now analyzed the central and privileged role of (reclining) free adult males in convivial ideology broadly, we can now direct our attention to women in particular.

III. WOMEN'S DINING POSTURE: LITERARY REPRESENTATIONS

This historical and ideological analysis of women's dining posture begins by surveying some literary texts that pertain to the question, roughly in chronological order. These texts range from Plautus to the high empire.[38] The visual representations, found again on funerary reliefs and in Campanian mural decoration (see sections IV–V below), all date from the mid first century C.E. onward. Literary texts, then, offer the only *contemporary* evidence for women's conviviality in the republican period. I devote special attention to this material in the next few pages for the following reason. The quotations with which we opened, from Varro (transmitted by Isidore) and Valerius Maximus, assert that in an

---

[37] These other houses are I.10.7, V.2.4, and VI.16.36. Certain dining scenes now in the Naples museum are without precise provenance, and others occur (with no discernible patterns of deployment) in grand houses.

[38] The practice and iconography of dining women at Rome, whether seated or reclining, is no doubt heir to both Greek and Etruscan practice and iconography. I cannot pursue these precedents here, but for starters see Fabricius 1999, 115–16, 169–73, 229–30, 284–86, 338–39, for women's dining postures in various Hellenistic cities of Asia Minor; also De Marinis 1961, 74–76, and Small 1994, 87–88, on their dining postures in various Etruscan cities. Yet Roman practice and representations must make cultural sense in Roman terms; it is this distinctively Roman cultural sense that I pursue in the following pages.

(undefined) early period, Roman women dined seated but subsequently took up the reclining convivial posture just as men did. I noted that, for over a century, scholars have accepted this account, though with some disagreement about the date of the postural transition—perhaps in the late republic, perhaps a generation or so later. The early literary evidence, therefore, looms disproportionately large, providing a test of this scholarly *communis opinio* and also, perhaps, of the antiquarian claims of Varro and Valerius themselves. To adumbrate my conclusion (section VI), I will argue that the *communis opinio* is quite wrong and that the historical status of the antiquarians' claim is at best unclear. What makes the antiquarian claim interesting, however, is not so much the (perhaps false) concrete information it conveys about who did what when, but rather the ideological effects and implications of making such a claim about how women behaved long ago.

Plautine comedy provides the earliest representations of women's dining posture in Roman literature—indeed, the earliest depictions of Roman dining *tout court*. Plautus stages a number of *convivia* in which prostitutes recline to dine alongside high-status males. Such events follow readily from the stock comic plot device whereby a well-born youth falls in love with a courtesan. Thus in *Asinaria*, a prostitute reclines to dine, sharing a couch with the father of the youth who loves her. The youth himself is present but reclining on another couch. Again in *Mostellaria*, a well-born youth reclines to dine with the prostitute he loves, though she is technically no longer a slave, as he has recently purchased her freedom. In the same scene, the youth's friend and his own prostitute arrive to share the meal, and they too recline together on a couch. *Bacchides* is filled with convivial situations in which the title characters—both prostitutes—recline with the two elite youths or their fathers.[39] Finally, an anecdote describing an historical event from this period activates all the same status relations, again in a convivial context. This anecdote relates that L. Quinctius Flamininus, discharging his consular (or perhaps proconsular) duties in Gaul or northern Italy in the late 190s B.C.E., summoned a condemned criminal to his dining room and had him cruelly executed there, because a *scortum* with whom he was reclining had asked to see a man killed.[40] Yet, while all of these passages

<hr/>

[39] *Asin.* 830–32, 878–79; *Most.* 308–9, 326–27, 341–43; *Bacch.* 79–81, 139–42, 754–58, 834–52, 1188–93, 1203–4.

[40] This anecdote, rooted in the historical tradition, was appropriated by the declaimers of the early empire and formulated as a *controversia*. Cic. *Sen.* 42 and Plut. *Cato Maior* 17.3 date the event to Flamininus' consulship (192 B.C.E.), while Sen. *Cont.* 9.2.2.pr. places

make the reclining woman a prostitute and pair her with an elite male on a dining couch, this is not the only possible combination. In Plautus' *Persa*, a male slave, Toxilus, reclines at a *convivium* with the prostitute he loves and whose freedom he has just purchased (763–67). Here, the woman's juridical status surpasses the man's, though in context this fact seems insignificant since Toxilus usurps the generic features of the young (elite) lover along with those of the clever slave and often exercises masterly authority over other figures (McCarthy 2000, 153–58). Conversely, a *convivium* in *Stichus* is populated entirely by slaves from the same *familia*. Here a woman reclines on a couch with two men (750–52). She is called an *ancilla* and implied not to be a prostitute.[41]

The relationship between Plautine representation and contemporary Roman social practice is (to say the least) difficult to sort out. For while Plautine drama assuredly engages contemporary Roman sociopolitical structures and norms, it also derives many plot devices, character types, and much of its formal structure from Greek New Comedy. Disentangling these strands is a tall order, given the dearth of other contemporary evidence.[42] Yet even if the juxtaposition of prostitutes and high-status males on dining couches is a stock comic situation with Greek roots, and even if elite youths fall in love with prostitutes far more predictably on the comic stage than in real life, nevertheless, Roman society itself included both elite males and prostitutes, and the comedies neither draw much attention to these pairings in *convivia* nor present them as transgressive. I therefore incline to think that these situations, as represented on stage, appeared unexceptional to contemporary Roman audiences and generally accorded with their own expectations about proper convivial behavior. The anecdote about Flamininus and the *scortum* independently supports this view, as it involves all the same status relations and social dynamics in an unambiguously Roman social context.[43] Moreover, we can conjecture what one pertinent convivial norm may have been in this period. Slaves, as we saw above (section II),

---

it in his proconsulship (191 B.C.E.; also apparently Livy 39.42.8, Val. Max. 2.9.3). The accounts vary regarding the sex of the *scortum* (woman or youth) and the status of the person executed (condemned criminal or prisoner of war).

[41] Stichus' outraged query *prostibilest tandem?* (765), when Sangarinus tries to steal a kiss from her, presupposes the answer "no."

[42] These are familiar lines of discussion in Plautine scholarship; for recent work, see McCarthy 2000, 17–29 (and *passim*), Anderson 1993, 133–51; Gruen 1990, 124–57.

[43] Certainly, Flamininus' *convivium* is presented as problematic and transgressive— but only because elements of elite *negotium* intrude inappropriately into a situation

function instrumentally in the Roman *convivium*, at least in later periods where the evidence is fuller. They normally manifest and perform their instrumentality by standing in service, but might assume some other posture if they thereby enhance the pleasure of the privileged, reclining diners. Prostitutes who recline alongside men to whom they provide sex are a clear instance of this. Thus these Plautine situations are consistent with what we know in general of how slaves functioned, both practically and ideologically, in other (later) Roman convivial contexts.

One passage in Plautus, however, complicates the picture. The title character of *Amphitruo* is an aristocrat, as he commands the army of the Greek city Thebes. His wife Alcmena is obviously no slave or prostitute, since it was both a Roman social reality and a key plot device in comedy that only the free could contract legal marriages; indeed, she must be elite herself, a social match for her husband.[44] Now, midway through the play, Amphitruo returns home after some months away on campaign. He greets Alcmena, only to find her insisting that he had already arrived the previous evening. She says that, upon arriving, he gave her a kiss (800) and bathed (802). Then they dined: *cena adposita est; cenavisti mecum, ego accubui simul* (804, cf. 735). Subsequently, she says, they retired together to bed. She implies clearly, and with enough emphasis to suggest considerable enthusiasm, that a sexual encounter followed (807–8). Now, the audience knows that last evening's "Amphitruo" was in fact Jupiter, disguised to seduce her. Consequently, the real Amphitruo grows increasingly alarmed at her story, anxiously asking *in eodem lecto?* when she says that they dined reclining together (answer: *in eodem*, 805). In fact, at every stage of this narration, one or another character underscores the erotic character of the progression from kissing, to reclining for dinner together, to having sex. The slave Sosia declares his "displeasure" with both the kiss and the dining (*non placet*, 801, 805), and Amphitruo himself declares, after Alcmena affirms that they spent the night together in the same bed (808–9), that she has "killed him" (*haec me modo ad mortem dedit*, 809) by losing her *pudicitia* in his absence (811). Here, then, as in the other Plautine passages, the posture of a woman who reclines to dine alongside a man has an erotic implication. It

---

otherwise constituted as *otium* (n. 12 above); the reclining prostitute herself helps to constitute the scene as "leisured."

[44] One aspect of her characterization as an elite is that, in reply to her husband's accusations of adultery, she appeals to her lineage: "istud facinus, quod tu insimulas, nostro generi non decet" (820).

is the middle element in a sexual crescendo that begins with a kiss and concludes with the couple having sex and sleeping together. Yet here, the woman shares the man's elite status, and in general a sexual symmetry seems to obtain, with Amphitruo (or Jupiter) being as much Alcmena's erotic object as she is his; the sexual pleasure to be had is distributed between the two.[45] This passage, then, implies that the practice identified above for elite males and prostitutes encompasses "respectable" women as well. It suggests that a wife would naturally recline to dine alongside her husband and that the audience would find such a practice familiar and unexceptional.

The next body of evidence dates from the late republic. In this period, too, we find women of diverse social and sexual statuses reclining alongside elite males at *convivia*. Certainly women of low status figure among these. In his second Catilinarian oration (*Cat.* 2.10), delivered in 63 B.C.E., Cicero invokes the specter of a debauched *convivium* in which wine-soaked, gluttonous, perfume-drenched followers of Catiline, exhausted by their illicit sexual exertions, embrace "shameless women" as they recline, plotting murder and fiery destruction for the city. Similarly, in a letter of 46 B.C.E., Cicero describes a *convivium* at the house of Volumnius Eutrapelus in Rome, attended by a number of male aristocrats, in which the actress and courtesan Cytheris was also present and reclining to dine: *infra Eutrapelum Cytheris accubuit . . . non me hercule suspicatus sum illam adfore* (*Fam.* 9.26.2). Bradley (1998, 47) explains that Cytheris reclined because "[s]he was an actress, and for a woman of her profession, or that of a *meretrix*, the conventions of respectable society did not apply," where by "conventions of respectable society," he presumably means the "strict protocol" (mentioned in the same paragraph), whereby the dutiful, subordinate wife sat while her husband reclined. Cytheris was assuredly not married to Eutrapelus but was his freedwoman and was almost certainly his sexual partner at one time or another.[46] Again, however, we must resist the temptation to associate the

[45] For Alcmena's enthusiastic recollection of the sex (Jupiter is apparently good in bed), compare 807–8 with 512–15, 735. The intimacies Alcmena describes are in her view perfectly unexceptional for a married couple: in response to Amphitruo's accusations, she asks uncomprehendingly, "quid ego tibi deliqui si, cui nupta sum, tecum fui?" (817, cf. 818; for *esse cum aliquo/a* meaning "to have sex with," see Adams 1982, 177).

[46] Cytheris as freedwoman of Eutrapelus: Serv. *ad* Verg. *Ecl.* 10.1. At the time of Cicero's letter, she is attested as Antony's mistress; she is later, famously, identified with "Lycoris" in the erotic elegy of Cornelius Gallus (for the sources, see Groß, "Volumnius (17)," *RE* 9A (1961): 883, with Laigneau 1999, 183–85). See also Treggiari 1991, 302, 305, on Cytheris, and Leach 1999, 150–53, on this letter.

reclining convivial posture exclusively with low-status women. In a queru-
lous letter to Atticus dating to 51 B.C.E. (*Att.* 5.1), Cicero describes the
rudeness of Atticus' sister Pomponia to her husband Quintus Cicero,
Marcus' brother, during a day the three spent together while traveling.
First, Marcus reports, she harshly rejected Quintus' suggestion that the
three collectively host a dinner. Then she refused to join the Cicero
brothers and their guests as they reclined for a meal and rejected food
that Quintus sent her from the table. Finally, to cap it all, she refused to
sleep with Quintus.[47] Marcus makes clear that at every stage Pomponia
behaved unreasonably, unsociably, and undutifully. He faults her, then,
not merely for refusing to recline with Quintus among the dinner company and then refusing to retire to bed with him. By commenting also on
the harshness of her words and on her rejection of food sent her from the
table, Marcus seems to invoke a larger social expectation or norm that
wives (at least elite ones) were equal partners with their husbands in the
pleasure and leisure of the *convivium*. They should enjoy the same nour-
ishment (hence the gesture of sending food), the same company and
conversation, and presumably the same sexual titillation (hence the expectation of retiring to bed together) that normatively characterize the
convivial experience for reclining men. These are precisely the expectations that Plautus' Alcmena invoked in conversation with her own
spouse.[48]

This Plautine and Ciceronian evidence begins to suggest a pattern.
Since, in all these passages, the woman who reclines (or is expected to
recline) alongside a man on a dining couch is known or likely to be
sexually attached to him, it is tempting to propose that the converse is
true: namely, a man and woman who recline together on the same couch
in a convivial setting thereby *signal* their sexual connection, regardless of

[47] Cic. *Att.* 5.1.3–4: "tum Quintus 'en' inquit mihi 'haec ego patior cottidie.' . . . idque
me ipsum commoverat; sic absurde et aspere verbis vultuque responderat. dissimulavi
dolens. discubuimus omnes praeter illam, cui tamen Quintus de mensa misit; illa reiecit.
quid multa? nihil meo fratre lenius, nihil asperius tua sorore mihi visum est . . . Quintus . . . .
Aquinum ad me postridie mane venit mihique narravit nec secum illam dormire voluisse et
cum discessura esset fuisse eiusmodi qualem ego vidissem."

[48] Other texts dating from or referring to the late republic that depict elite women
reclining to dine alongside their husbands, or imply that this convivial practice was the
norm, are Cic. *Ver.* 2.5.80–82, Suet. *Aug.* 70, and especially Dio Cass. 48.44. To my knowledge, Treggiari 1991, 423, is the only scholar to observe (correctly) that elite married
women in the late republic are regularly attested as reclining to dine alongside their
husbands; others (as at n. 3 above) assert that women began reclining no earlier than the
Augustan period.

the woman's status. Such a partnership presents itself as "licit"—i.e., involving a man and women who can have sex without *stuprum*. "Licit" relationships range from marriage proper to quasi-marital relationships (*concubinatus* or *contubernium*), to the sexual use of one's own or others' slaves, to prostitution.[49] Conversely, it is a grave transgression if a couple who cannot have licit sex reclines together to dine, for their posture and juxtaposition would be taken to imply that they do, nevertheless, have sex and so are guilty of *stuprum*.[50] This interpretation is incompatible with the scholarly *communis opinio* (itself an interpretation of Varro and Valerius) that "respectable" women dined seated in the republican period. I suggest, rather, that any women not precluded under the rubric of *stuprum*, including both "respectable" ones (i.e., wives) and "non-respectable" ones (e.g., prostitutes), could and did dine reclining along-side their male sexual partners, thereby visibly affirming the existence and social legitimacy of that partnership. Nevertheless, crucial differences remain between women at the high and low ends of this social spectrum. Slave prostitutes, for instance, being inherently instrumental to the pleasure of the privileged, reclining males, can only have reclined on the males' sufferance and only if they thereby made an especially significant contribution to the males' convivial pleasure (e.g., by charging up the erotic atmosphere or providing entertainment). Presumably they could be reduced to standing in service, or be required to do something entirely else, at any time. At the other social extreme, elite wives, in reclining alongside their husbands in *convivia*, thereby participated substantially or fully in the leisure and various pleasures of the event. They benefited from the slaves' attention no less than their husbands; they shared the same food, drink, entertainment, and erotic subjectivity as

---

[49] *Stuprum* is the moral and legal category with respect to which Romans defined the "forbidden" and "permitted" sexual partners for men and women of various statuses. See Williams 1999, 96–103, (and his chap. 3 *passim*) on *stuprum*, along with Treggiari 1991, 299–309, on women who are "fair game" for elite males; also, McGinn 1998, 194–202, on the legal codification of these longstanding social conventions under Augustus.

[50] The trick played on Nicobulus in Plaut. *Bacch.* relies on this expectation. Nicobulus is led to believe that the unknown woman with whom he sees his youthful son reclining to dine is another man's wife, a "forbidden" category of woman. Nicobulus immediately infers that his son's life is in danger, since the couple could be killed as adulterers by the woman's husband should they be discovered (*Bacch.* 832–71)—an inference requiring the presupposition that reclining to dine together implies a sexual connection (cf. 892–97, where this assumption is made explicit). In fact, Nicobulus' inference about the sexual connection is correct: he is deceived only about the status of the woman who is actually a prostitute and therefore a licit sexual partner for the youth.

their husbands; and—on the evidence of Pomponia—they substantially controlled their own level of engagement, far from being automatically subject to their husbands' commands or wishes. What modes of partici- pation might have been available to a socially intermediate figure like Cytheris—neither a slave nor a wife, but a freedwoman who socialized at the highest levels of elite male society—is less clear, though we catch sight of her reclining alongside her patron and (probable) sexual partner, apparently participating fully.

Representations of women's conviviality become more plentiful in Augustan and imperial texts. These representations confirm that a woman's dining posture—at least in elite male company—expresses her sexuality, but they show considerable ambivalence about the consequences of such expression. Especially striking are several tableaux in Ovid's elegiac poetry where the male lover, reclining in a *convivium*, observes his beloved reclining on another couch with another man and plots to se- duce her. In *Amores* 1.4, the woman in question is explicitly described as reclining alongside a man, the image of her "warm[ing] the breast of another, placed close below him" (*alteriusque sinus apte subiecta fovebis?* v. 5), and the other gestures of intimacy that the poet-lover observes or fears that the two may exchange (vv. 4–6, 15–16, 29–30, 33–44) suggest that readers would understand this couple as reclining in close physical contact, with the man at the head of the couch and the woman slightly toward the foot, her back against his chest. That is, he reclines above her (in the high position on the couch) and she below him (in the low position). Clearly, this positioning facilitates physical contact, among other things.[51] The lover, for his part, proposes a set of signals that he and his beloved might exchange, across the distance that separates them, to signify their attraction and perhaps set up a tryst. A similar tableau in the *Heroides* (16.217–58) depicts a banquet in Sparta in which the hosts, Helen and Menelaus, recline together on a couch exchanging various physical intimacies, while Paris, their guest, watches enviously from an- other couch. Here, too, the sexually charged atmosphere made possible by mixed-sex reclining on a dining couch is vividly portrayed.[52] In a third

---

[51] This is the usual ordering of mixed-sex couples in wall paintings that show conviv- ial scenes: see fig. d, with discussion below.

[52] Menelaus and Helen are never explicitly said to recline together. But Paris says he himself is reclining (16.233, 257), and Menelaus, too, must be assumed to be reclining as the host and as an elite male. Moreover, the constant kissing and touching between husband and wife (16.221–26) indicates they are adjacent to one another and resembles the contact made between the woman and her *vir* in *Am.* 1.4. Helen, too, then, seems to be reclining and sharing a couch with her husband.

passage, *Ars Amatoria* 1.565–608, Ovid presents these same convivial practices and social dynamics in a didactic mode: he advises his reader how to proceed if, at a *convivium*, he should notice an attractive woman reclining on another couch alongside another man.

Certain patterns remarked in the republican material persist in these Ovidian representations. First, the couples who recline together are connected in sexual relationships that the various diners seem to accept as "legitimate," including the lover himself, whatever his designs on the woman.[53] Second, the women, whatever their status, seem to be full and equal participants with the men, again sharing the food, wine, companionship, posture, and sexual subjectivity of their male partners. Third, these texts continue to suppose, at least in many cases, that couples who recline to dine together will subsequently retire to bed for sex.[54] Yet these texts also reveal a new dimension of the sociosexual politics of women's dining posture. For in these passages, the sexuality that a woman displays while reclining with a man is not completely contained by that relationship. Rather, it spills out and infuses the whole *convivium*, creating the anxiety (or hope) that she may become sexually available to other men. Thus, the elegiac texts make clear that a woman's normal placement on the couch below her man, with her back to his chest, not only facilitates physical contact between them, but also enables him to keep her under surveillance.[55] Nevertheless, these texts credit her with numerous resources by which she and a lover reclining on another couch can stymie his surveillance, so as to make approaches and responses to

---

[53] Whether such couples in elegiac poetry can be considered *truly* "legitimate"—i.e., involving no *stuprum*—is uncertain, since the precise social status and circumstances of the elegiac beloved is notoriously difficult to pin down (see McKeown 1989, II 78, I 19–24; Treggiari 1991, 303, 306). My point, rather, is that the *rhetoric* (verbal and postural) of legitimacy normally attaches to these couples, and the lover accordingly presents himself as a seducer. In a very few cases, the couple's relationship is specified: in the *Heroides* passage Helen and Menelaus are married, while in Prop. 4.8, the poet-lover reclines alongside two prostitutes on a couch to dine (vv. 27–34)—no *stuprum* in either case.

[54] The poet of *Am.* 1.4 foresees that the reclining couple will have sex after the *convivium* (59–70); likewise in Prop. 4.8, where the lover's declaration that he sought "unfamiliar passion" (*Venere ignota*, 34) in Cynthia's absence, hired two prostitutes (29–33), and reclined to dine with them (37–44) can only mean that he expected sex to follow. Also, Paris, as he observes the intimacies of Helen and Menelaus on the dining couch (*Her.* 16.221–28), knows that they "have sex throughout whole nights" (*heu facinus! totis indignus noctibus ille / te tenet, amplexu perfruiturque tuo, Her.* 16.215–16).

[55] Thus the man reclining above "his" woman observes her secret signs to another lover at Ov. *Am.* 2.5.13–28 and *Ars Am.* 2.549–50.

one another: writing signs or letters in wine on the tabletop; drinking from the same part of a cup as the lover does, when cups of wine circulate around the party; getting the man with whom she reclines drunk so he falls asleep, whereupon she and the lover can communicate more openly.[56] Accordingly, the liaisons that she and the lover seek out are adulterous or quasi-adulterous, undercutting the claim to sexual exclusivity, legitimacy, and recognition made by the reclining posture and dining couch she shares with "her" man. These lover's trysts therefore occur at other times and other places, away from the *convivium* and its couches, and so do not assert legitimacy for themselves by this means.[57]

The hope (or fear) that the woman who reclines below a man on a dining couch, thereby expressing a legitimate sexual connection to him, may also generate an excess of erotic energy that extends transgressively beyond this man to encompass other men, is not just a figment of the hypereroticized elegiac imagination. Traces of this idea appear in texts of other genres, in both the Augustan and imperial age. We hear of one Gabba feigning sleep during a *convivium* so that his wife could flirt with Maecenas, who reclined elsewhere. We also hear of the young Octavian taking the wife of a consular, before her husband's eyes, out of the dining room and into a bedroom, returning her shortly with flushed face and disheveled hair. Caligula, too, is said to have taken other men's wives from the triclinium for sex.[58] In each case, presumably, the wife in question was reclining on a couch below her husband in accordance with the legitimate sexual connection and as a full, equal participant in the leisure and pleasures of the *convivium*.

Occasionally, even this postural rhetoric of legitimacy might be enlisted in the service of sexual transgression. Caligula broadcast the fact that he committed *stuprum* with his sisters by having them recline below him on his couch during *convivia* (as if this sexual connection were legitimate), while his wife was displaced to the position above.[59] Like-

---

[56] For such strategies, see (e.g.) Tib. 1.6.15–20, 27–28; Ov. *Am.* 1.4.11–32, 51–58; *Ars Am.* 1.565–78; *Her.* 16.249–54. In all of these passages the woman is explicitly said, or clearly implied, to be reclining below a man. See also Yardley 1991.

[57] For the circumstances of such trysts, see e.g. Ov. *Ars Am.* 1.603–8; *Am.* 1.4.45–50.

[58] Gabba: Plut. *Mor.* 759F–60A. Augustus: Suet. *Aug.* 69.1. Caligula: Suet. *Cal.* 25.1, 36.2; Sen. *Const.* 18.2. Cf. Hor. *Carm.* 3.6.23–28; Plin. *Nat.* 14.141. Still other imperial texts where women recline to dine: Vitr. *Arch.* 6.7.4; Mart. *Epig.* 10.98.1–6; Tac. *Ann.* 4.54; Petr. 67.1–5 (note here Fortunata's supposed reluctance to join the party, in contrast to Habinnas' expectation that she will; note too that she constantly moves around the dining room and never alights anywhere for long; cf. §§37.1, 52.8–10, 54.2, 70.10).

[59] Caligula and his sisters: Suet. *Cal.* 24.1, "cum omnibus sororibus suis consuetudinem stupri fecit plenoque convivio singulas infra se vicissim conlocabat uxore supra cubante."

wise, Tacitus reports (*Ann.* 11.27) that Messalina and her lover C. Silius
brought their adulterous liaison into the public eye not only by celebrat-
ing a wedding ceremony (though she was still married to Claudius) but
also by reclining together on a couch at the wedding banquet, and then
(in normal fashion) retiring to their "conjugal" bed for sex. In these
passages the diners are assuredly sexually transgressive, but not by virtue
of pursuing sexual encounters outside of the legitimate relationship symbolized by the joint reclining posture. Rather, they co-opt and subvert
this very symbol of legitimacy itself.

One circumstance under which the potential for transgression may
be realized is the heavy consumption of wine. According to Dionysius of
Halicarnassus (2.25.6), Romulus determined that women who committed adultery or drank wine should be put to death, since "adultery was
the beginning of madness, and drunkenness the beginning of adultery."
Valerius Maximus (2.1.5) gives a similar account of this early prohibition.
Ovid declares in several places that wine dispels worries and makes
lovers bolder, and Pliny the Elder laments in general terms the harm,
including adultery, wrought by excessive convivial drinking.[60] Still other
texts from a range of periods speak of adultery and drunkenness in
almost the same breath, thereby betraying the close conceptual connection between them, even without drawing an explicit causal link.[61] Scholars have explained this alleged Romulean prohibition on women drinking wine in various ways.[62] For our purposes, what matters is that the
convivium could be considered all the more likely a locus for sexual
transgression precisely because women had, or could have, access to
wine there.

In fact, this "Romulean" prohibition on women drinking wine further illuminates the claim of Valerius and Varro that early Roman women
were forbidden to dine reclining. For these prohibitions are two sides of
the same ideological coin. Each betrays an anxiety about the potential
for women's sexuality to escape the bounds of social legitimacy and to

---

Caligula seems to be imagined as the middle diner on a three-person couch, though
possibly he could be at the head of a two-person couch with his wife "above" him in the low
position of the couch above (so Hurley 1993, 97).

[60] Ov. *Ars Am.* 1.241–44, 3.762; *Her.* 16.231–32, 243–48; Plin. *Nat.* 14.141. Similarly,
Sen. *Ep.* 85.20.

[61] E.g., Cic. *Cat.* 2.10; Val. Max. 6.3.9; Gell. 10.23.3, along with the fragment of Cato
the Elder in Gell. 10.23.4.

[62] For a collection of the crucial texts and survey of earlier scholarship, see Pailler
2000; also Bettini 1995; Minieri 1982.

move from licit, overtly declared connections to illicit, secretive ones that qualify as *stuprum*. Each asserts that such movement was stymied—i.e., women's sexuality was properly regulated—in a remote, morally valorized past. For it is "long ago," or "in the reign of Romulus," that women neither drank wine nor dined reclining. Each prohibition implies or concedes that the mechanism no longer operates in the morally fallen present. Each, finally, points to the *convivium* as a locus of particular anxiety, the situation most liable to give rise to and foster a woman's impulse to sexual transgression, whether because she reclines alongside a man or because she drinks wine there. In the terms set out in section I above, then, we see that Varro and Valerius—indeed, the literary material as a whole—foregrounds the ideological (rather than historical) dimension of women's dining posture. It is the social, sexual, and more broadly cultural meanings and values tied up with her posture that are most visible and susceptible of analysis. Nevertheless, this material hardly leaves us bereft of historical information, and to this we return in the conclusion (section VI below).

Even this analysis is only partial, however. For while the numerous and varied literary representations of women who dine reclining enable us to pinpoint some of that posture's socioethical implications, we have no idea (so far) what the *seated* posture might mean, the posture that Varro and Valerius attribute to early women and that is otherwise virtually unattested in literary texts (but see n. 76 below). Yet the seated posture is no mere fantasy, for it appears with some regularity on early imperial funerary monuments. To proceed with our ideological analysis of women's dining posture, then, we turn to the visual evidence and to funerary monuments first.

IV. WOMEN'S DINING POSTURE AND FAMILY VALUES ON SUB-ELITE FUNERARY MONUMENTS

Like the grave altar of Calpurnius Beryllus discussed above (fig. a), and indeed like all funerary monuments bearing convivial reliefs for which the evidence is clear, the two discussed in this section commemorate, and one was dedicated by, freed persons or persons of undistinguished freebirth (e.g., the children of freedmen). They therefore provide a different ideological engagement with dining from that found in the literary texts examined above, which manifest the convivial concerns and values of elite males (whatever the status of the women with whom they recline).

Consider an ash-urn dating to perhaps the 60s or 70s C.E. in the

Palazzo Corsini in Rome (fig. b, S 276) on which a dining scene is sculpted in relief, a scene iconographically close to that of Beryllus. Here a woman reclines in the classic dining posture on a couch with lowish endboards and backboard.[63] She appears to hold a piece of fruit in her left hand, rather than a drinking vessel, but this does not mean that wine is unavailable to her. For near the foot of the couch (an unusual position) stands the familiar three-legged table with zoomorphic legs on which rests a drinking vessel, a mixing vessel, and a ladle. Above the table, in mid air, hovers a loaf of bread or cake. Thus both food and drink, the essentials of conviviality, are represented. The woman wears a mantle around her hips and legs, like Beryllus, and it is unclear whether her torso is clothed in a thin tunic or is (like his) entirely nude. If nude, then she too is costumed in the unrealistic manner that idealizes the leisure and pleasures of the *convivium* and "heroizes" the diner.[64] Around the couch stand three figures of childlike stature and proportions. The two standing near the head wear short tunics resembling those worn by Beryllus' slaves; the one in the foreground holds a doll or perhaps a bird, while the one behind perhaps adjusts the woman's pillow. The third stands behind the couch near the foot, holding a long curved object above the reclining woman—perhaps a flapping piece of fabric with which he fans her.[65] While these figures are surely slaves, they are not the sexually desirable, adolescent male variety that attend upon Beryllus.

[63] Though this figure appears to have a visible breast and female hairstyle, its sex may nevertheless be debatable, since the inscription commemorates a man: De Luca 1976, 119, no. 64, carefully calls it a "figura" without ever ascribing a sex to it, while Sinn 1987, 160, no. 276, and Altmann 1905, 145, no. 160, both see a woman. However, the shoes under the couch are paralleled only for monuments that show women reclining alone, e.g., on the urns of Lorania Cypare (S 462, shoes rest on footstool) and Iulia Capriola (S 516; Candida 1979, 74–76, no. 31, and pl. 26). Such shoes are never found on reliefs showing men reclining alone or men and women reclining together. Thus they seem to indicate the female sex of the figure under discussion here.

[64] Any such nudity should present her as Venus (see below for another such iconographic motif); for a woman with a clearly nude torso and hip mantle on a dining relief, see the late second-century *loculus* cover from Isola Sacra discussed and illustrated by Amedick 1991, 136, no. 84, and Taf. 3.2 (also 20: "die . . . Frau . . . ist gleich Venus mit entblößtem Oberkörper dargestellt"). On the other hand, our woman on S 276 may be wearing a very thin tunic, such as that of Lorania Cypare (S 462, who also wears a mantle covering her lower body).

[65] Sinn 1987, 160, no. 276, identifies the objects as a doll and a fan; De Luca 1976, 119, no. 64, sees a bird. For slaves fanning reclining diners see Varone 1993a, 640 (cf. n. 36 above), and Mart. *Epig.* 3.82.10–12.

Rather, these are younger, prepubescent children. A handful of literary passages describe or allude to child-slaves kept by elite women—slaves considered desirable for their innocence, childish antics, and talkativeness, even impudence.[66] The slaves represented on this monument, and on several other monuments commemorating women, may be child-slaves of this sort.[67]

Here, it seems, is confirmation in an early imperial, sub-elite social context (we have already seen it in elite literary texts) that the convivial pleasures available to free men and women are generally parallel. For this monument's iconography closely parallels that of Beryllus in that each diner reclines alone on the couch and is represented as enjoying various pleasures and luxuries of idealized elite dining and drinking. Each diner has his or her every need attended to by attentive slaves who themselves signal luxury and wealth, and the diners may (or may not, depending on the woman's costume) share an idealizing nudity. Nor is this monument unique; several other sub-elite monuments from the first and second centuries C.E. show women reclining to dine alone on a couch, with or without slave attendants.[68] As a group, these closely parallel a series of similar monuments commemorating males and so suggest that there is no great distinction between male and female enjoyment of convivial leisure and pleasures. In only one respect do these monuments show a gender differentiation: Beryllus' slaves are of the sexually attractive, adolescent male variety that elite males stereotypically desire, while the woman's are of the adorable, impudent, prepubescent variety that elite women stereotypically collect. This iconographical difference implies at least one differentiation in convivial pleasures. The slaves on Beryllus' monument are presumably his sexual objects and give his convivial pleasure an erotic component, while those on the woman's monument probably enhance her convivial experience in other, nonsexual

[66] For such slaves, see especially Dio Cass. 48.44.3. They may also be associated with women in elegiac and lyric poetry, as Slater 1974, 136–37, argues: e.g., perhaps in Cat. 55, 56, 58; Prop. 2.29A (assimilated to *erotes*); and Tib. 1.5.26. They are also sometimes associated with men, as at Suet. *Aug.* 83 (and further passages at Slater 133–35).

[67] Other such monuments: S 462, with such children left, right, and behind the couch; S 458, with such children left and right of the couch (the togate child seated on the couch must be freeborn); and a plaque in Geneva (*loculus* cover? Chamay-Maier 1989, 80) with a very small long-haired child in a tunic sitting on the foot of the woman's couch. In general on child-slaves and their hair, see Fless 1995, 56–63; Amedick 1991, 19–22; Slater 1974, 135–38.

[68] In addition to the monuments listed in the previous note, see B 8 and S 516.

ways. This difference is subtle, however, and the scenes remain parallel in most respects. Indeed, the fact that the deceased, whose name is recorded on the inscription, is male—a freedman named M. Servilius Hermeros[69]—may not mean that the dedicator made a terrible mistake when purchasing this urn. Supposing that no dining scene with a male figure and adolescent slaves were available, the female figure with child slaves might have been considered close enough, since in all other respects the iconography of elite, leisured, luxurious dining, and the social integration that this iconography communicates, is similar.

But when a man and woman are depicted *together* in a convivial funerary relief, this iconographical symmetry breaks down. On such monuments, the man reclines at the head of the couch, while the woman, almost invariably, is represented as seated on the couch's foot. Here, finally, on funerary monuments that postdate Varro and Valerius by several generations, we encounter scenes that look like what these authors describe as the convivial practice of the remote past. Let us examine one such monument in detail. An altar of middling size in the Vatican (fig. c; B 327, 94 x 66 x 39 cm), of Flavian or Trajanic date, displays a relief in which a man reclines in the classic dining posture, a drinking vessel in his left hand. The couch has the usual back and curved endboards. Before him stands the usual table with zoomorphic legs, holding several further vessels. His gaze is directed toward the foot of the couch. There, on the edge of the couch, sits a woman whose body and gaze are correspondingly oriented toward him. Though her right arm is broken off above the elbow, her right hand survives, clasped with his in the *dextrarum iunctio* gesture, which in some cases accompanies a marriage connection. Both figures are clothed in tunics and mantles (no "heroizing" nudity here). His costume may be the elusive *synthesis* or dining-suite, or more probably the outer garment is a toga (a *balteus*-like curve extends from his left shoulder to right hip), by which he would be asserting his citizen status. Her mantle, meanwhile, may notionally be draped over her left arm in the manner of a *palla* that sometimes seems to connote modesty and chastity, though there is no sign of the *stola*, the matronal garb *par excellence*.

Beneath this relief is an inscription naming the deceased as P. Vitellius Successus and the dedicator as his wife Vitellia Cleopatra, both, undoubtedly, freed persons or the children of freed persons of the same

---

[69] *M Servilio M et Ɔ lib / Hermeroti pio / im patrono suo / vixit annis L* (*CIL* VI 36337).

gens.[70] Inscription and image fit together impeccably: the *dextrarum iunctio* of the couple on the couch is consistent with marriage, and the portrait-heads borne by these figures are reproduced in a second pair of portraits in the pediment that crowns the altar. This couple must surely be the couple named in the inscription. What, then, of the woman's posture? Evidently, it marks a degree (at least) of inferiority to the reclining man. She does not share his posture of ease; moreover, the table, with the pleasures of wine and food that it represents, is located much more conveniently to him than to her, and while he holds a drinking vessel in his left hand, her left hand is empty. In short, she appears rather less than a full and equal participant in the leisure and pleasures her husband enjoys. On the other hand, she does at least share his couch, and as a married couple they undoubtedly have a sexual connection. Further-more, were slaves present in this scene, she would enjoy their ministra-tions no less than he, and her position in the social hierarchy—as well as in the hierarchy of postures—would be more readily perceived as "inter-mediate": inferior to the reclining man, yet by no means reduced to the instrumentality of those who stand in service.[71]

Several other funerary urns and altars bear dining scenes similar to this one, and in one case standing slaves are also present.[72] But in no case is the reverse configuration found: never does a woman recline while a man sits. Moreover, this arrangement is invariable regardless which mem-ber of the couple is deceased and regardless who dedicates the monu-ment; that is, the man *as such* monopolizes the reclining posture,[73] and the gender-differentiated postures correspond to differential enjoyment

---

[70] *Dis Manibus / P Vitelli Sucessi /Vitellia Cleopatra / uxor bene merenti / fecit* (*CIL* VI 29088a). For detailed art-historical discussion of this monument, see Kleiner 1987, 158–60, and an excellent photo of the dining scene at pl. xxvi.

[71] Adult males, too, are occasionally said to sit in *convivia*, their posture marking their social inferiority to higher-status men who recline: see Plaut. *Stich.* 486–93; Suet. *Poet.* fr. 11.27–33; Dio Cass. 59.29.5; also, Cic. *Ver.* 2.3.62 for an elite male humiliated by being made to stand.

[72] See B 833 (reclining man, seated woman, standing slaves); B 775, 784, 955, S 457 (all showing a reclining man and seated woman, but no slaves).

[73] On monuments where a single figure reclines on a dining couch—man or woman—it is generally clear that the reclining figure represents the deceased. But when a man and woman appear together, she sits and he reclines regardless whether he is deceased and she dedicates to him (B 327, the Vitellii just discussed; also S 457); or she is deceased and he dedicates to her (B 775); or he or a third party dedicates the monument for both of them (B 784, B 955). On B 833, the man dedicates to himself, and the woman is epigraphically invisible.

of convivial pleasure. Why should this be, when literary texts consistently portray wives (or their equivalent) as reclining alongside their men, having full access to the food and wine, and generally participating equally in the leisure and pleasures of conviviality? I propose an explanation that returns to an association of female reclining discussed above: the idea that, by reclining alongside a man and so announcing a licit sexual connection, she also exudes a sexual energy that may extend transgressively beyond this licit connection to encompass other men, an effect further enhanced by wine drinking. Recall that the sub-elites who dedicate these monuments are appropriating an image of elite conviviality as a symbol of, or means of claiming for themselves, social integration and belonging. Yet such persons have particular, status-specific concerns that also demand iconographical expression. Urban freedmen of the late republic and Augustan era, for instance, usually chose a different way of asserting their social belonging on funerary monuments. They emphasized, iconographically as well as epigraphically, the juridical existence and emotional solidarity of their family ties. The men are represented wearing togas (stressing their juridical status as free citizens and their capacity both to contract legal marriages and raise legitimate children); spouses clasp hands; women make the *pudicitia* gesture; children wear togas and *bullae*.[74] Although the funerary iconography of urban freedmen evolved in new directions in the early empire, some of these earlier devices persisted and are found in the dining scenes examined here (e.g., the likely toga and the *dextrarum iunctio* seen on the altar of the Vitellii, fig. c).

Here, then, is the crux: these two strategies for asserting social belonging—assuming an elite convivial guise and stressing the existence and solidarity of familial ties—do not mesh perfectly. The elite convivial practice whose image these freedmen sought to appropriate included the figure of the woman reclining and drinking wine alongside her man. But the potential for sexual transgression associated with the reclining woman could seem incompatible with these freedmen's equally strong desire to insist that the couple shared an exclusive, legally recognized marriage bond (which implies their juridical status as free citizens).[75] This problem could, however, be resolved by the stratagem of representing the woman

---

[74] See Zanker 1975, 279–94 on these funerary monuments, the *Fenstergucker* type of the late republic and Augustan era.

[75] Any hint of sexual promiscuity might also be redolent of the sexual use to which they themselves, or their parents, had been put as slaves.

seated at the foot of the couch, with the man reclining at the head. The overall atmosphere of elite conviviality is little compromised by this distortion of actual elite practice. Meanwhile, the woman's posture and position separates her from the man's body and from the dangerous wine on the table before him (and again, *she* never holds a drinking vessel), thereby eliminating the more intense eroticism, and transgressive overtones, of the woman who reclines and drinks wine with a man. Nor do monuments showing women who recline *alone* on a dining couch (such as the Hermeros monument, fig. b) tell against this argument. For the absence of a man sharing her couch minimizes the erotic overtones of such scenes, notwithstanding the woman's horizontality and (in some cases) wine drinking. Anxieties about *stuprum* or adultery in particular emerge only insofar as her body relates to a male body. The seated woman, then, I interpret as a sub-elite adaptation of the imagery of elite conviviality, one that accommodates their particular (and distinctively non-elite) concern to assert their juridical status through a display of familial bonds.

Iconographical analysis, then, clarifies the moral significance of the woman who dines seated while her man reclines, a significance that Valerius and Varro leave unexplained when they (merely) imply that the posture denotes traditional womanly virtue.[76] Whether Roman women of any status actually dined seated in any period, we discuss in the conclusion (section VI).

V. WOMEN'S DINING POSTURE AND SUB-ELITE SELF-REFLECTION IN POMPEIAN PAINTING

If the above explanation is correct—namely, that a status anxiety distinctive to sub-elites accounts for why, on funerary monuments, they depict

[76] Aside from Varro and Valerius, I know only two literary texts representing women who dine seated while their men recline—both cited by Bradley 1998, 47, and both dating from the late first or second century c.e. In Dio Chr. *Or.* 7.65, this is the convivial practice of an idealized Greek peasant household; in Apul. *Met.* 1.21–22, it is that of a miserly Thracian moneylender. Both texts thus depict values and practices *remote* from those of contemporary, elite, urban Romans (likewise Varro and Valerius, who locate this practice in a distant, morally valorized past). The distinctively non-elite concerns of urban freedmen, manifested in the distinctive convivial iconography on their funerary monuments, only corroborates the impression left by these literary texts: that the practice of women dining seated, and its associated values, are remote from elite urban ways and not (*contra* Bradley 1998, 47) the proper practice for elites at any time.

woman as dining seated in male company—then we may wonder why the same posture is not seen in our other corpus of sub-elite convivial representations, namely, the dining scenes painted in dining rooms of sub-elite Pompeian houses. One such painting was discussed above (section II) with emphasis on how the experience of the men is articulated iconographically. We saw that, in general, these men are shown enjoying the same sorts of (characteristically elite) convivial pleasures as the men on the funerary monuments and as the elite males in many literary texts. But if we reexamine these paintings with an eye to the women's convivial experience, we find that this experience resembles that portrayed in texts but differs from that represented on the funerary monuments. In this section I seek to pinpoint these differences and account for them in their particular social setting.

We begin by considering anew the painting from the west wall of the *triclinium* in the bakery and residential complex at IX.12.6–8 (see n. 32 above). I argued that this painting depicts two of the familiar pleasures of elite conviviality in a heightened form: overt representations of intoxication and the heightened erotic charge of women reclining against the men's bare chests. These features take on a new aspect, however, now that we have examined the socioethical implications of women's dining posture. First, in light of the literary evidence analyzed in section III, the women in this scene, who recline below men on dining couches, may be interpreted as sharing with them a licit sexual connection (i.e., one involving no *stuprum*). Indeed, the men with their "idealizing" but also erotically bare torsos, against which the women press their shoulders, seem no less the women's sexual objects than the women are theirs, since the partners share horizontality and full-body contact (not to mention idealized youth and beauty). This collocation also, as the Ovidian passages show, enables the couple to touch, caress, and exhibit other signs of their sexual connectedness before the eyes of the assembled party. Second, the women enjoy the ministrations of the slave no less than the men do—here, in fact, the standing woman monopolizes the slave's attention, at least for the moment. Third, since these women recline alongside the men, the tables that bear drinking implements are equally convenient (or inconvenient) to both. Indeed, the fact that every women in this scene clutches a wine cup, and two are overtly intoxicated, indicates that they share fully the pleasures of wine with the men—for the man on the middle couch is himself presumably asleep from wine. In all these respects, then, these women (like those in the literary texts) seem to be full participants in the leisure and pleasures on offer in this *convivium*. Yet we have seen that women's wine drinking, especially in *convivia*, was stereotyped as tending toward adultery or other sexual transgression, for the woman who reclined *and* drank alongside a man was thought capable of generating a sexual "excess" that could draw in other men. So while this scene shows no obvious sexual transgressions in progress, it displays a number of the attested predictors, or proximate causes, of such transgressions.[77]

This eroticism is even more overt in another painted scene that exists in two versions: one from the north wall of this same dining room, and the other (fig. d) now in the Naples Museum, but of uncertain provenance originally.[78] Here, two couples recline on couches, the women below their bare-chested men. These couples share a tall, three-legged table with hoofed feet, which holds a small silver drinking service. The woman on the rightmost couch clutches a large silver drinking vessel, and in figure d looks to her left toward a cooling vat that holds still more wine (in the Casti Amanti painting, a slave stands to the far right, pouring wine into this vat). The sunshade overhead indicates that this convivial event occurs outside. A bit of forest is visible to the left, wherein a flute-player and another slave take a break from their own toils. A statue of a god (probably; Varone 1993a, 627–28), holding a staff, presides over the event. For our purposes, the striking feature of this scene is the couple kissing passionately on the leftmost couch, the woman's left shoulder pressed to her man's chest.[79] Moreover, her *tunica* is falling off her right shoulder and has drifted well down toward her elbow, leaving her shoulder, upper arm, and a portion of her right breast visible. This "drooping garment" motif derives from the iconography of Venus and is fairly common in paintings and sculpture of the first and second centuries C.E. (indeed, Vitellia Cleopatra—the seated wife in figure c—has a similarly

---

[77] A similar analysis can be applied to several other Campanian wall-paintings showing dining scenes: one on the east wall of this same dining room (Varone 1993a, 640, cf. n. 36 above); one on the north wall, discussed immediately below; a scene found in two copies—one from dining room (8) in I.10.7, and the other from an unknown room in VIII.2.38–39; also, the scene from the north wall of triclinium (r) in V.2.4. See also a scene known in three closely related versions: triclinium H of VI.16.36; room 12 of VI.9.2/13; and MNN 9024, from an unknown location in Herculaneum.

[78] This panel, MNN 9015, has traditionally been assigned to a small workshop in Pompeii (I.3.18), but this assignment is now known to be incorrect (Varone 1997, 149). Its provenance is therefore completely unknown. For the panel from IX.12.6–8, see Varone 1993a:639, and image no. 6 on the website given in n. 32.

[79] This kiss is paralleled in at least one (MNN 9193) and maybe a second (MNN 9207) small scene of erotes and psyches banqueting, from triclinium 16 of IX.3.5/24: see *PPM* IX 275 fig. 196, and 267 fig. 188, respectively.

exposed right shoulder).[80] This is yet another "idealizing" motif that, like the nude torso, places the figure so depicted in a slightly elevated sphere, imbuing her and the *convivium* as a whole with the values and characteristics associated with this goddess. Among these, of course, are physical beauty and sexual allure. The drooping garment both implies and puts before a viewer's eyes these attributes of the woman so represented.

The overt eroticism of the couple's kiss and the sagging tunic again calls to mind the highly eroticized *convivia* constructed by the Augustan elegists, which provide a literary analog to the iconography of these paintings. While these two forms of representation are unlikely to have a direct connection (I do not hold that the paintings "illustrate" elegiac *convivia* or that the elegists "narrate" scenes like these), they do share a rhetorical stance toward conviviality. Both present an ironized, exaggerated, even parodic image of certain potentialities inherent in any standard, mixed-sex *convivium*. Any Roman would probably agree that a woman who reclines to dine below a man thereby declares her sexual connection to him. But the elegists and paintings constantly submit to their audiences that, especially when combined with drinking wine, this sexuality becomes especially pronounced, producing excess and transgression. Thus these particular representations are attention-grabbing and amusing because they depict a recognized potential as being substantially *realized*—an extreme result that is probably quite unlike the normal unfolding of actual *convivia*.

Turning to these paintings' social context—a dining room in a house/bakery, in which a prosperous but sub-elite proprietor probably hosted primarily his social equals and inferiors at *convivia*—we may wonder what meanings the viewers found in them. Since sub-elites from the city of Rome, at roughly this same time, were employing funerary monuments bearing convivial reliefs that show women sitting in male company, and since (as I argued) this gendered differentiation of postures responds to the anxieties of the dedicators *qua* sub-elites regarding the possibility of sexual promiscuity, then why would such persons shed these anxieties when decorating their dining rooms and represent women not only reclining to dine alongside men, but kissing them, drinking heavily, losing their garments, and generally exuding a transgressive sexuality?

One answer may reside in the self-reflexivity of the viewing situation—the fact that these paintings, showing men and women reclining

---

[80] On this motif as Aphrodisiac, see Kleiner 1981, 520; Wrede 1971, 128, and more generally, D'Ambra 1996. Literary parallels: Ov. *Ars Am.* 3.307–10; Tib. 1.6.18.

together on couches in a *convivium*, were painted on the walls of a dining room to be observed by men and women who reclined together on couches in a *convivium*. A handful of literary texts from the late republic and early empire describe people who encounter and interpret paintings. These passages, which cannot be discussed at length here, tend to depict Roman viewers as making meaning out of paintings by seeing them as commentaries on their own immediate situation.[81] If so, then the self-reflexive viewing situation discussed here—dining scenes painted in dining rooms—would seem only to confirm and strengthen that impulse. It seems likely that the diners who viewed these scenes examined them at least in part for how they compare to the actual *convivium* unfolding in that very room in which they themselves were participating. On the one hand, the paintings show ideally beautiful and youthful (for the most part) men and women, dining in surroundings that range from comfortable to grandiose. Thus the diners are presented with an idealized image of the luxury in which their social superiors dine, a desirable image likely to outshine their own, more modest, material surroundings. On the other hand, the rather exaggerated, even parodic depictions of heightened female sexuality and general intoxication might cause the viewers to question whether these are models of elite deportment that socially insecure sub-elites would actually want to adopt. In this respect the diners might not wish to "jump into the picture," or transform the actual *convivium* into a simulacrum of the picture, so as to inhabit these roles for themselves. While we can never know all the ways in which an individual might find meaning in a painting, it seems likely that status-anxious sub-elites might have constructed meaning, *inter alia*, in the two domains just defined: on the one hand material luxury as a proxy for social status, and on the other hand personal conduct also as a proxy for social status. "I'll take the furniture, but leave the behavior" might well be the verdict of the aspiring sub-elite as she or he dines under these scenes. Funerary monuments, in contrast, differ both in their social context and in their modes of articulating belonging. By their nature, such

[81] Ter. *Eun.* 583–92 (Chaerea is inspired to rape his beloved, upon viewing a painting of Jupiter approaching Danae in a golden shower); Plut. *Brut.* 23 (Porcia, preparing to leave Brutus, identifies with Andromache in a painting of Hector's departure); Petr. 83 (Encolpius interprets scenes of divine-human love matches as emphasizing divine blessedness, in contrast to his own misery); Verg. *Aen.* 1.453–93 (Aeneas *literally* finds himself in the mural of the Trojan war in Juno's temple at Carthage and takes the scene to be "about" himself and his situation). For this kind of reception of painting, see Zanker 1999 and Fredrick 1995.

monuments concern families, whether in commemorating family groups or in being dedicated by spouses, children, or parents. These monuments put the family forward as a vehicle for claiming status, and for sub-elites (as we have seen) this means affirming familial solidarity. In the funerary context, the desired status claims could be made by toning down those aspects of elite conviviality that suggest female sexual transgression (hence women sit in male company). However, the status-conscious self-reflection at which the mural decoration aims is best achieved by *exaggerating* those same potentially transgressive elements.

VI. CONCLUSION: HORIZONTAL WOMEN IN IDEOLOGY AND PRACTICE

This article opened by distinguishing two questions emerging from the antiquarian claims of Varro and Valerius Maximus, both of whom assert that Roman women dined seated in the good old days, while conceding that they no longer dine seated in the (morally degenerate) present. First, a historical question: what posture or postures did women of various status in fact assume in Roman *convivia* at various times? Second, an ideological question: what were the social, ethical, and political implications of a woman assuming one convivial posture or another? Partial answers to these questions have appeared in the subsequent analyses of three broad categories of evidence for women's conviviality, namely, literary texts, Roman urban funerary monuments, and Campanian wall paintings. It is now time to collect these partial answers and fill in some remaining gaps.

The literary evidence as a whole, we observed, provides abundant resources for addressing the ideological question. First, it shows that the reclining posture symbolizes many of the same things for women as for men: *otium*, privilege, and pleasures of various sorts (e.g., gustatory, vinolent, conversational, sexual). Beyond this, many literary representations make women's dining posture a proxy for matters of sexual propriety in general. We can now further assert that the visual representations discussed in sections IV and V also provide plentiful resources for the ideological inquiry. These images confirm that reclining women share broadly the same leisure and pleasures as reclining men. But each corpus of images also problematizes, in its own way, the matter of sexual propriety. On the funerary monuments, to deny a woman the reclining posture and depict her as seated in male company was to deny even a hint of sexual promiscuity on her part—an important claim for sub-elites. In the mural decorations, again directed primarily at sub-elites, to represent a woman as reclining and drinking alongside a man was to raise precisely this specter of sexual promiscuity and thus to raise the question of what constitutes correct (status-marked) convivial deportment.

But what of the historical question? I argued in section III that the earliest representations of women's conviviality—all literary, mostly Plautine—probably accord with contemporary convivial norms when they portray women of various statuses reclining to dine alongside elite males with whom they had a "licit" sexual connection. This is assuredly the convivial norm in the late republic, the Augustan era, and the early empire. From this period, so many texts of so many different sorts portray women reclining to dine alongside elite males (when not precluded under the rubric of *stuprum*) that normative practice cannot possibly have been otherwise. This does not mean, of course, that all women dined reclining all the time. Slave women standing in service at a *convivium* would not ordinarily recline, and even women for whom reclining was the norm (e.g., wives) may have had the option to do otherwise— Pomponia, recall, withdrew altogether. Nevertheless, the *communis opinio*, which interprets Valerius and Varro to mean that women (at least "respectable" ones) regularly dined seated, not reclining, in male company at least through the late republic, and possibly beyond, is assuredly wrong. Valerius and Varro might be vindicated if they are taken to refer to a period *preceding* any for which we have contemporary evidence, i.e., before Plautus. But I strongly suspect that they transmit no factual information whatsoever about early practice. Rather, they retroject into the morally valorized past the opposite of the practice they observe in their own, morally fallen day. For them, as for many others, women's dining posture is principally a proxy for women's sexual mores.

The visual material raises a somewhat different historical question, since it emerges from and addresses itself to a *uniformly* lower-status social milieu, where the men as well as the women are mostly freed persons or of low freebirth. Is it possible that in this milieu women actually did, normatively, dine seated on the foot of the couch on which their husbands reclined, thereby making in real life the social and ideological claims that their funerary iconography made for them after death? Alas, it is extremely difficult to infer actual social practice from the funerary monuments or wall paintings, or indeed from the few literary texts that depict the conviviality of low-status free persons.[82] However, if

---

[82] Literary evidence: Dio Chr. *Or.* 7.65 and Apul. *Met.* 1.21–22, which describe sub-elite *convivia* in which the women sit, are overtly speaking of Greeks (see n. 76 above); it

diners saw these paintings as commentaries on their own immediate situation, as I proposed above, women could perhaps do so more easily if they were themselves reclining, just as the women in the paintings do. Moreover, the funerary monuments that show women reclining on a couch alone (as in fig. b) may likewise imply that women generally reclined in this social milieu, even in male company. For given what we know of freedmen's social preoccupations, it seems easier to understand why women who actually dined reclining should be represented on funerary monuments as sitting in male company, than to understand why women who actually dined sitting should be represented on some monuments as reclining alone. That is, funerary monuments tend to be conservative, so funerary representations seem more likely to depict distinctly conservative practices (more conservative than real life, anyway) than to depict distinctly radical ones. Indeed, the image of the seated woman can hardly have served across social strata as an ideologically potent symbol of antique sexual restraint and virtue if the practice was actually familiar and widespread in those social strata. Thus, ideology can illuminate social practice by indicating what is presupposed or taken for granted. So, despite disagreeing with Keith Bradley on certain specifics (see n. 76 above), I agree with him generally in distinguishing the ideology of women's dining posture from the practice while acknowledging their interrelation. This fundamental observation opens the way for further culturally attuned interpretations not only of convivial posture but of other bodily deportments as well, thus enabling us to write new chapters in the histories of dining, gender, and the body in the Roman world.[83]

THE JOHNS HOPKINS UNIVERSITY
e-mail: mroller@jhu.edu

---

is hard to know how, if at all, we can relate such representations to actual sub-elite Roman conviviality. Petronius extensively describes a freedmen's convivial milieu, and there the women do (sometimes) recline when present in the room (see n. 58 above). But whether the behavior of Fortunata and Scintilla are representative of actual sub-elite female conviviality in general is far from clear.

[83] I thank Thomas Habinek, Michael Koortbojian, Alan Shapiro, Herica Valladares, and two anonymous referees for their engaged and critical readings of earlier versions of this paper; also, audiences at Yale, Johns Hopkins, and the 2002 meeting of the AIA/APA for their critiques of oral versions. Photo credits: fig. a: after Altmann 1905, 153, fig. 124; fig. b: photo Rossa, Deutsches Archäologisches Institut, neg. no. 74.727; fig. c: after Altmann 1905, 192, fig. 154; fig. d: after Herrmann-Bruckmann 1904, Taf. 210.

ABBREVIATIONS

B = Boschung 1987 (followed by catalogue no.)
MNN = Museo Nazionale Archeologico, Naples (followed by inventory no.)
PPM = G. Pugilese Carratelli and I. Baldassarre, eds. *Pompei: Pitture e Mosaici.*
Istituto della Enciclopedia Italiana. 10 vols. to date, 1990– .
S = Sinn 1987 (followed by catalogue no.)

BIBLIOGRAPHY

Adams, J. N. 1982. *The Latin Sexual Vocabulary.* Baltimore: Johns Hopkins University Press.
Allison, Penelope M. 2001. "Using the Material and Written Sources: Turn of the Millennium Approaches to Roman Domestic Space." *AJA* 105:181–208.
Altmann, Walter. 1905. *Die römischen Grabaltäre der Kaiserzeit.* Berlin: Weidmann'sche Buchhandlung.
Amedick, Rita. 1991. *Die Sarkophage mit Darstellungen aus dem Menschenleben.* Berlin: Gebr. Mann.
Anderson, W. S. 1993. *Barbarian Play: Plautus' Roman Comedy.* Toronto: University of Toronto Press.
André, Jean-Marie. 1966. *L'otium dans la vie morale et intellectuelle romaine des origines à l'époque augustéenne.* Paris: Presses Universitaires de France.
André, Jean-Marie, et al., eds. 1996. *Les loisirs et l'héritage de la culture classique.* Brussels: Latomus.
Astbury, Raymond, ed. 1985. *M. Terenti Varronis Saturarum Menippearum Fragmenta.* Leipzig: Teubner.
Balsdon, J. V. P. D. 1962. *Roman Women.* London: Bodley Head.
Bettini, Maurizio. 1995. "In vino stuprum." In Murray and Tecusan, 224–35.
Boschung, Dietrich. 1987. *Antike Grabaltäre aus den Nekropolen Roms.* Bern: Stämpfli & cie.
Bradley, Keith R. 1987. *Slaves and Masters in the Roman Empire: A Study in Social Control.* Oxford: Oxford University Press.
———. 1998. "The Roman Family at Dinner." In *Meals in a Social Context*, ed. Inge Nielsen and Hanne Sigismund Nielsen, 36–55. Aarhus: Aarhus University Press.
Candida, Bianca. 1979. *Altari e cippi nel Museo Nazionale Romano.* Rome: Giorgio Bretschneider.
Chamay, Jacques, and J.-L. Maier. 1989. *Art romain: Sculptures en pierre du Musée de Genève*, vol. 2. Mainz: Philipp von Zabern.
Christenson, David, ed. 2000. *Plautus Amphitruo.* Cambridge: Cambridge University Press.
D'Ambra, Eve. 1996. "The Calculus of Venus: Nude Portraits of Roman Matrons." In *Sexuality in Ancient Art*, ed. Natalie Boymel Campen, 219–32. Cambridge: Cambridge University Press.

D'Arms, John. 1991. "Slaves at Roman Convivia." In *Dining in a Classical Context*, ed. William Slater, 171–83. Ann Arbor: University of Michigan Press.

———. 1995. "Heavy Drinking and Drunkenness in the Roman World: Four Questions for Historians." In Murray and Tecusan, 304–17.

———. 1999. "Performing Culture: Roman Spectacle and the Banquets of the Powerful." In *The Art of Ancient Spectacle*, ed. Bettina Bergmann and Christine Kondoleon, 301–19. New Haven: Yale University Press.

De Luca, Gioia. 1976. *I monumenti antichi di Palazzo Corsini in Roma*, 2 vols. Rome: Accademia Nazionale dei Lincei.

De Marinis, Simonetta. 1961. *La tipologia del banchetto nell'arte etrusca arcaica*. Rome: Giorgio Bretschneider.

Dentzer, Jean-Marie. 1982. *Le motif du banquet couché dans le Proche-Orient et le monde grec du VIIe au IVe siècle avant J.-C.* Rome: École française de Rome.

Dexheimer, Dagmar. 2000. "Portrait Figures on Funerary Altars of Roman *liberti* in Northern Italy: Romanization or the Assimilation of Attributes Characterizing Higher Social Strata?" In *Burial, Society and Context in the Roman World*, ed. John Pearce et al., 78–84. Oxford: Oxbow Books.

Dickmann, Jens-Arne. 1999. *Domus frequentata: anspruchsvolles Wohnen im pompejanischen Stadthaus.* Munich: Dr. Friedrich Pfeil.

Dunbabin, Katherine M. D. 1993. "Wine and Water at the Roman *convivium*." *JRA* 6:115–41.

———. 1996. "Convivial Spaces: Dining and Entertainment in the Roman Villa." *JRA* 9:66–80.

Edwards, Catherine. 1993. *The Politics of Immorality in Ancient Rome.* Cambridge: Cambridge University Press.

Fabricius, Johanna. 1999. *Die hellenistischen Totenmahlreliefs: Grabrepräsentation und Wertvorstellungen in ostgriechischen Städten.* München: Dr. Friedrich Pfeil.

Fless, Friederike. 1995. *Opferdiener und Kultmusiker auf stadtrömischen historischen Reliefs. Untersuchungen zur Ikonographie, Funktion und Benennung.* Mainz: Philipp von Zabern.

Förtsch, Reinhard. 1995. "Villa und *Praetorium*. Zur Luxusarchitektur in frühkaiserzeitlichen Legionslagern." *Kölner Jahrbuch* 28:617–28.

Foss, Pedar. 1994. "Kitchens and Dining Rooms at Pompeii: The Spatial and Social Relationship of Cooking to Eating in the Roman Household." Ph.D. diss., University of Michigan, Ann Arbor.

Fredrick, David. 1995. "Beyond the Atrium to Ariadne: Erotic Painting and Visual Pleasure in the Roman House." *Classical Antiquity* 14:266–87.

Galsterer, Brigitte and Hartmut. 1975. *Die römischen Steininschriften aus Köln.* Cologne: Greven & Bechtold.

Ghedini, Francesca. 1990. "Raffigurazioni conviviali nei monumenti funerari romani." *Rivista di archeologia* 14:35–62.

Gruen, Erich S. 1990. *Studies in Greek Culture and Roman Policy.* Leiden: E. J. Brill.

————. 1992. *Culture and National Identity in Republican Rome.* Ithaca: Cornell University Press.

Habinek, Thomas. 1998. *The Politics of Latin Literature.* Princeton: Princeton University Press.

Heskel, Julia. 1994. "Cicero as Evidence for Attitudes to Dress in the Late Republic." In *The World of Roman Costume*, ed. Judith Lynn Sebesta and Larissa Bonfante, 133–45. Madison: University of Wisconsin Press.

Herrmann, Paul (continued by Reinhard Herbig). 1904. *Denkmäler der Malerei des Altertums.* Munich: F. Bruckmann (plates by Bruckmann).

Himmelmann, Nicolaus. 1973. *Typologische Untersuchungen an römischen Sarkofagreliefs des 3. und 4. Jahrhunderts n. Chr.* Mainz: Philipp von Zabern.

Hölscher, Tonio. 1987. *Römische Bildsprache als semantisches System.* Heidelberg: Carl Winter.

Hopkins, Keith. 1983. *Death and Renewal.* Cambridge: Cambridge University Press.

Hurley, Donna. 1993. *An Historical and Historiographical Commentary on Suetonius' Life of C. Caligula.* Atlanta: Scholars Press.

Jones, Henry Stuart. 1912. *A Catalogue of the Ancient Sculptures Preserved in the Municipal Collections of Rome*, 2 vols. Oxford: Clarendon Press.

Kay, N. M. 1985. *Martial Book XI: A Commentary.* New York: Oxford University Press.

Kleiner, Diana E. E. 1981. "Second-Century Mythological Portraiture: Mars and Venus." *Latomus* 40:512–44.

————1987. *Roman Imperial Funerary Altars with Portraits.* Rome: Giorgio Bretschneider.

Koortbojian, Michael. 1995. *Myth, Meaning and Memory on Roman Sarcophagi.* Berkeley: University of California Press.

Laigneau, Sylvie. 1999. *La femme et l'amour chez Catulle et les Élégiaques augustéens.* Brussels: Latomus.

La Penna, Antonio. 1995. "Il Vino di Orazio: nel *modus* e contro il *modus.*" In Murray and Tecusan, 266–82.

Leach, Eleanor Winsor. 1999. "Ciceronian 'Bi-Marcus': Correspondence with M. Terentius Varro and L. Papirius Paetus in 46 B.C.E." *TAPA* 129:139–79.

Ling, Roger. 1995. "The Decoration of Roman *Triclinia.*" In Murray and Tecusan, 239–51.

Marquardt, Joachim, and August Mau. 1886. *Das Privatleben der Römer*, 2d. ed. (1st ed. of 1879 by Marquardt; 2d by Mau). Leipzig: S. Hirtzel.

McCarthy, Kathleen. 2000. *Slaves, Masters, and the Art of Authority in Plautine Comedy.* Princeton: Princeton University Press.

McGinn, Thomas A. J. 1998. *Prostitution, Sexuality, and the Law in Ancient Rome.* New York: Oxford University Press.

McKeown, James C. 1989. *Ovid, Amores: Text, Prolegomena, and Commentary in Four Volumes.* Liverpool: Francis Cairns.

Minieri, Luciano. 1982. "Vini usus feminis ignotus." *Labeo* 28:150–63.

Mols, Stephan T. A. M. 1999. *Wooden Furniture in Herculaneum: Form, Technique, and Function.* Amsterdam: Gieben.

Murray, Oswyn. 1985. "Symposium and Genre in the Poetry of Horace. *JRS* 75:39–50.

Murray, Oswyn, and Manuela Tecusan, eds. 1995. *In Vino Veritas.* London: British School at Rome.

Neraudau, Jean-Pierre. 1984. *Être enfant à Rome.* Paris: Les Belles-Lettres.

Pailler, Jean-Marie. 2000. "Quand la femme sentit le vin." *Pallas* 53:73–100.

Painter, Kenneth. 2001. *The Insula of the Menander at Pompeii. Volume IV: The Silver Treasure.* Oxford: Clarendon Press.

Richardson, Lawrence, Jr. 1988. *Pompeii: An Architectural History.* Baltimore: Johns Hopkins University Press.

Richter, Gisela M. A. 1966. *The Furniture of the Greeks, Etruscans and Romans.* London: Phaidon Press.

Sinn, Friederike. 1987. *Stadtrömische Marmorurnen.* Mainz: Philipp von Zabern.

Slater, William J. 1974. "Pueri, turba minuta." *BICS* 21:133–40.

Small, Jocelyn Penny. 1994. "Eat, Drink, and Be Merry: Etruscan Banquets." In *Murlo and the Etruscans: Art and Society in Ancient Etruria,* ed. Richard D. De Puma and Jocelyn Penny Small, 85–94. Madison: University of Wisconsin Press.

Toner, J. P. 1995. *Leisure and Ancient Rome.* Cambridge: Polity Press.

Treggiari, Susan. 1991. *Roman Marriage: Iusti Coniuges from the Time of Cicero to the Time of Ulpian.* Oxford: Clarendon Press.

Varone, Antonio. 1993a. "Scavi recenti a Pompei lungo via dell'Abbondanza (*Regio* IX, *ins.* 12, 6–7)." In *Ercolano 1738–1988, 250 anni di ricerca archeologica,* ed. Luisa Franchi dell'Orto, 617–40. Rome: Giorgio Bretschneider.

———. 1993b. "New Finds in Pompeii: The Excavation of Two Buildings in Via dell'Abbondanza." *Apollo* 138 no. 377:8–12.

———. 1997. "Pompeii: Il quadro Helbig 1445, «Kasperl im Kindertheater», una nuova replica e il problema delle copie e delle varianti." In *I temi figurativi nella pittura parietale antica (IV sec. a.C. - IV sec. d.C.). Atti del VI convegno internazionale sulla pittura parietale antica,* ed. Daniela Scagliarini Corlàita, 149–52. Bologna: University Press.

Wallace-Hadrill, Andrew. 1994. *Houses and Society in Pompeii and Herculaneum.* Princeton: Princeton University Press.

Wardle, D. 1994. *Suetonius' Life of Caligula: A Commentary.* Brussels: Latomus.

Weaver, P. R. C. 1967. "Social Mobility in the Early Roman Empire: The Evidence of the Imperial Freedmen and Slaves." *Past & Present* 37:3–20.

Williams, Craig A. 1999. *Roman Homosexuality: Ideologies of Masculinity in Classical Antiquity.* New York: Oxford University Press.

Wrede, Henning. 1971. "Das Mausoleum der Claudia Semne und die bürgerliche Plastik der Kaiserzeit." *MDAI(R)* 78:125–66.

Yardley, John C. 1991. "The Symposium in Roman Elegy." In *Dining in a Classical Context*, ed. William Slater, 149–55. Ann Arbor: University of Michigan Press.

Zaccaria Ruggiu, Anna Paola. 1995. "Origine del triclinio nella casa romana." In *Splendida civitas nostra: studi archeologici in onore di Antonio Frova*, 137–54. Rome: Quasar.

Zanker, Paul. 1975. "Grabreliefs römischer Freigelassener." *JDAI* 90:267–315.

———. 1988. *The Power of Images in the Age of Augustus*. Trans. Alan Shapiro. Ann Arbor: University of Michigan Press.

———. 1999. "Mythenbilder im Haus." In *Proceedings of the XVth International Congress of Classical Archaeology, Amsterdam, July 12–17, 1998*, ed. R. F. Doctor and E. M. Moormann, 40–48. Amsterdam: Allard Pierson Museum.

TOWARD A TYPOLOGY
OF ROMAN PUBLIC FEASTING

JOHN F. DONAHUE

Abstract. The categories associated with modern French commensality help to illuminate various forms of Roman public dining, most notably, meals linked to events of the life cycle and religious festivals, as well as those sponsored by *collegia* and by the emperor himself. A comparative approach of this sort brings into sharper focus the nature of this social practice by underscoring the propensity of meals in the ancient world both to unite and to separate diners by social rank.

INTRODUCTION

THE PURPOSE OF THIS ESSAY is to examine Roman public feasting during the Principate (where the sources are most plentiful) within the context of modern typologies of commensality in order to understand more fully the nature of this ancient social practice. The study of food has attracted much scholarly attention over the past decade. In the field of classical studies alone, much useful work has been done on upper-class dining and social relations, food in Roman literature and art, and in the related areas of the Roman food-supply system, public distributions, and food crises.[1] Even so, while certain types of Roman feasts, such as the formal dinner (*cena*) and public banquet (*epulum, convivium publicum*) have received treatment,[2] little attempt has been made to study Roman

---

[1] The bibliography on food and dining is too vast to be included here; instead, the works below represent the most useful studies of specific areas. On upper-class dining and social relations, see D'Arms 1984, 327–48; food in literature: Gowers 1993; Hudson 1993, 204–19; art: Dunbabin, 1993, 132, fig. 19 (Bardo mosaic of a feast in progress; for its identification as an *epulum*, see Slater, 1991, 136, and n. 102); Dunbabin 1999, 26–27 (for a mosaic depicting food remains, probably second century C.E.); food supply system: Aldrete and Mattingly 1999, 171–204; food and money distributions: Mrozek 1987; van Berchem 1975; food crises: Garnsey 1990, 126–46; Garnsey 1988.

[2] On the formal *cena*, see D'Arms 1990, 308–20; on the *epulum*, see, e.g., Pudliszewski 1992, 69–76. See also Dupont 1999, 113–27.

public banquets in a way that will bring them into sharper focus by explaining not only their form but also their deeper social function. The approach examined here has the advantages of weaving a wide cross section of Roman *testimonia* into a coherent (if imperfect) framework of festal typologies, while using a cross-cultural approach that can enrich our understanding of the ancient evidence.

Specifically, I will examine Roman public feasting in light of the typologies recently offered by Claude Grignon.[3] A sociologist with research interests in the food habits of modern France, Grignon has proposed categories into which various forms of French dining can be placed. Based largely on the recognition that the sharing of food inevitably leads to the forming of social relationships, which, in turn, help to determine the morphology of a particular dining experience, his analysis offers a useful starting point for exploring various types of Roman feasting as well.

At the same time, it is necessary to note some important qualifications. First, Grignon's focus is limited to modern France. The result is a work that is "probably oriented (and limited) by my own preoccupations."[4] Consequently, any larger connections to be made must be drawn from other times and cultures. Second, as a sociologist, Grignon is primarily interested in studying processes of interaction and patterns of collective behavior; he is less concerned with my present objective of fitting the dining experience into a larger historical framework, as a classicist or ancient historian might be. Even so, his emphases have much to offer in a Roman context and will receive careful consideration in the analysis to follow. Third, Grignon has appealed to his colleagues in other disciplines, historians and anthropologists, to "criticize and broaden" his analysis.[5] The present essay will attempt to take a step in this direction, with the ultimate goal of underscoring the important place of the public feast in Roman daily life.

SOCIAL MORPHOLOGY AND TERMINOLOGY

Before I examine the proposed typologies, I want to make two preliminary points. First, Grignon closely links commensality, the act of consum-

---

[3] See Grignon 2001, 23–33. For a fuller discussion of much of the evidence for Roman public feasting cited in support of Grignon's typologies in this paper, see Donahue 2004.

[4] See Grignon 2001, 25.

[5] See Grignon 2001.

ing food and drink together, with pre-existing social groups. According to this view, a given society comprises any number of such groups, which, in turn, are typically based on diverse criteria: age, gender or ethnicity; voluntary associations that are religious or political in nature; lineage or local origin; and, status or position within the social hierarchy. Furthermore, the multiplicity and diversity of these groups directly account for the wide variety of festal forms observable in any culture; hence, we have the presence of family dinners, meals that cluster around certain holidays or events of the life cycle, and meals open only to certain exclusive groups. As Grignon sees it then, the study of commensality is really about the study of "social morphology" in any given society.[6] In other words, in determining a particular typology of festal expression, we need to look at groups.

On the surface, this may strike the reader as rather self-evident. After all, how can one talk about sharing the table without talking about a group? It is in a Roman context, however, where this characterization becomes especially pertinent. Collectivist activities, after all, were a defining feature of the Romans, who routinely bathed and exercised, watched spectacles, and transacted business in each other's company. As we shall see in greater detail below, the Roman feast reveals a similar emphasis, as it was able both to bring people together in the Roman world and to amplify social differences among the diners. This set of circumstances is critical to understanding the dynamics of the Roman feast and, when examined in conjunction with elements such as the time, place, and participants of a particular eating event, it greatly enhances our understanding of the nature of social relations in the ancient world.[7]

Another issue is the distinction between commensality and conviviality. Grignon views the latter as the "manifestation of euphoria" that can accompany group eating, not as something synonymous with commensality itself. According to this interpretation, conviviality must be understood as the actual *result* of commensality, even if it is often times the more interesting and colorful of the two activities. In essence, it is simply a by-product of the larger process of sharing food and drink, with its characteristic emphasis on internal hierarchies and social groupings. Grignon argues that the two terms must not be confused, as is often the case.[8]

---

[6] See Grignon 2001, 24–25.
[7] On time, place, participants, etc., see Farb and Armelagos 1980, 4.
[8] See Grignon 2001, 24.

Although Grignon offers no exempla to underscore this claim, it is instructive to assess it within a Roman context. Here, what is most striking is the fact that, as in many modern instances, the Romans, too, sometimes displayed a certain imprecision over festal terminology. A simple case in point would be the apparent overlap (and even inter-changeability) in meaning between *convivium*, the Latin term for a fes-tive gathering, and *epulum*, the most common term for feast, seen most often in the usage of *convivium publicum* and *epulum/epulum publicum*. A further complicating factor is that terms such as these appear most frequently in epigraphic form within honorary and dedicatory inscrip-tions, where they tend to be used formulaically with few or no accompa-nying details. As a result, it is often difficult to distinguish one type of meal from another, or even whether a term signifies a meal or a cash handout to purchase a meal.[9] While the Romans may have been aware of shades of meaning among such terms, from a modern perspective one is hard pressed to detect substantive differences, and we are inevitably led to wonder if the ancient writers employed such terms interchangeably to designate meals that were essentially similar. When assessed in light of the Roman evidence, Grignon's observations about imprecision over festal terminology suggest that we are dealing not with an isolated mod-ern phenomenon but one that persists across time and cultures and that we must remain mindful of the distinctions—as well as the possible ambiguities—among the terms for different kinds of festal activity.

In turning to the proposed typologies, we find five categories of dining: (1) institutional, (2) domestic, (3) exceptional, (4) segregative, and (5) trangressive. Institutional commensality, which Grignon associ-ates with hospitals, nursing homes, barracks, jails, convents, and boarding houses, does not readily fit with the Roman evidence, while Roman domestic commensality, linked to family and private life, falls outside of our purview. Rather, I wish to focus on the latter three categories, since they more readily find analogues in the Roman evidence. Here, we shall be dealing primarily with public meals, that is, those to which the *populus* at large or specifically designated groups from the community were invited.[10] This survey will encompass meals across a broad spectrum of settings and circumstances and, at the same time, confirm the function of the shared meal both to unite and to classify its celebrants by social rank in the Roman world (a key component of modern typologies as well).

[9] On the issue of meals versus cash handouts, see Slater 2000, 107–22.

[10] Of course, the question of public and private in the Roman world is quite complex, meriting further treatment than can be reasonably offered here. For a fuller discussion, see Riggsby 1997, 36–56; more generally, Wallace-Hadrill 1994.

EXCEPTIONAL COMMENSALITY

Meals Associated with Events of the Life Cycle

Group eating has long been associated with ritual ceremonies of the life cycle.[11] Among the modern evidence, such occasions include Christmas, New Year's Day, or Easter meals, as well as celebration meals for births, comings of age, marriages, and funerals. Here, too, we find those meals associated with the world of work—occasions such as meals or parties to celebrate promotions or departures.[12] But while Grignon restricts this "intensive and remarkable commensality" to the extended family and their friends,[13] the Romans frequently attached a public aspect to these sorts of feasts that was perfectly consistent with the larger scheme of Roman social relations during the Principate. We see this in the coming-of-age ceremony (at which boys assumed the *toga virilis*), most notably when Octavian provided a festival for the citizenry at public expense, or, for the same type of occasion, when a certain priest of Tiberius provided a more modest repast of pastry and sweet wine (*crustulum et mulsum*) to the *populus* of Surrentum.[14] Marriages, too, were linked with public feasting (*cena nuptialis*). When Elagabalus married in the third century C.E., he invited the entire population of the city to drink freely.[15] Closely related to this ceremony was the birthday (*dies natalis*) of the emperor, on which occasion the *fratres Arvales* offered a sacrifice and feasted. That the larger *populus* feasted, too, is evident in Augustus' enactment of 12 B.C.E., which allowed unmarried men and women, who had been previously excluded, to partake in banquets on his birthday.[16]

And then there is death. We note especially the public funeral

[11] On ritual ceremonies of the life cycle, see Myerhoff 1982, 109; Cressy 1997; in a Roman context, see D'Arms 1984, 337.

[12] See Grignon 2001, 27–28.

[13] Grignon 2001, 27.

[14] On Octavian, see Dio Cass. 48.34; priest of Tiberius: *CIL* 10.688; for similar evidence, see *AE* 1994.345.

[15] On Elagabalus, see Dio Cass. 79.9. Equally significant is the *cena aditialis*, a meal offered by a priest upon assuming office. See Macrob. *Sat.* 3.13.10–12 and Taylor 1942, 385–412. The extravagance of this meal is well documented. Varro (*R.* 3.6.6) records that the orator Quintus Hortensius served peacocks for the first time on this occasion, and Seneca (*Ep.* 95.41) remarks that this *cena* could cost a million sesterces even for the stingiest of men. This sum need not be taken at face value, of course; nonetheless, the sentiment is revealing.

[16] On the *fratres Arvales* in general, see Scheid 1990a, 1990b; Beard 1985, 114–62; Syme 1980; on Augustus's enactment of 12 B.C.E., see Dio Cass. 54.30.5.

(*funus publicum*), a popular occasion for public feasts and games and, as a consequence, a tool to increase aristocratic competition and power. More than two hundred inscriptions and a handful of literary sources record public funerals in Rome and the West.[17] The evidence goes at least as far back as 328–27 B.C.E., beginning with a *visceratio*, a distribution of meat from a sacrificial carcass.[18] Over time, the benefactions for the *populus* increased, and the custom continued throughout the Republic and into the Principate, when such funerals were restricted to the emperor and members of his family. In this context, we must also include meals related to the *dies violaris* (day of violets) or the *dies rosalis* (day of roses). Named for the memorial flowers left on graves, these occasions typically involved an annual family gathering to remember a departed member. They took on a public aspect, however, when an individual established an endowment to provide a public feast each year on the anniversary of the deceased.[19]

In all this evidence, feasting underscores the relationship between benefactor and beneficiary, whether it is the interaction between the emperor and the urban *populus* or a wealthy patron and his townsmen. The primary motive of such benefactions was not public charity (although this was often the result of such largess) but the continual need to confirm publicly one's status. These occasions of the life cycle provided a convenient setting for fulfilling such aims. This is not to suggest, however, that these occasions completely lost their private aspect. But what becomes clear is the way in which these types of meals were monopolized by the emperor at Rome[20] and, following his lead, by elites in the surrounding municipalities.

Meals Associated with Religious Festivals

Within this sphere of exceptional commensality we must also include feasts linked with religious ceremonies. As was true in Greece, Roman religion was always more concerned with integrating its rituals within the

---

[17] For the most recent study, see Wesch-Klein 1993. In general, *RE Suppl.* 3, s.v. "funus publicum," cols. 530–32.

[18] On the *visceratio*, see Kajava 1998, 109–31.

[19] *Collegia* were especially popular as beneficiaries. See, e.g., *CIL* 5.2176, 11.126, 11.132 for instances related to the *dies rosalis*.

[20] Of course, this is true of the emperor's role in alimentary programs as well. See Garnsey 1968, 367–81; *OCD* 1996, s.v. "alimenta," 63.

broader patterns of everyday life than with the personal fulfillment of its followers. We find this to be the case in the various celebrations of the annual calendar, celebrations that offer great insight into the intersection of eating and ritual in Roman society. Even so, with regard to banquets at these celebrations, the Roman evidence is less enlightening than we would like.

Feasts connected with modern holidays such as Christmas and Easter recall several Roman celebrations offered on similar occasions throughout the year. No fewer than eight festivals of the Roman religious calendar included feasts among their activities, although of these, only two, the Saturnalia and the Compitalia, offered feasts that were truly open to the public at large. Opening with a great sacrifice at the temple of Saturn, the Saturnalia concluded with a banquet (*convivium publicum*) for all.[21] The Compitalia included a feast whose Roman version during the early Principate consisted of a procession, sacrifice, and *ludi scaenici* hosted by each of the city's neighborhood districts. The banquet itself was characterized as a "greasy crossroads feast" with "unappetizing fare" and "slimy water," a vivid reminder of its modest plebeian origins.[22]

Several additional Roman religious festivals included banquets that were restricted to certain political or social groups. Two of the most ancient and widely recognized of all Roman festivals, the *Ludi Romani* and *Ludi Plebeii*, included not only processions, sacrifices, and games but also the *epulum Iovis*, a feast in honor of Jupiter.[23] This was celebrated on the Ides by the *septemviri epulonum*, a special class of priests, who sacrificed purified oxen in the presence of the images of Jupiter, Juno, and Minerva resting on a couch (*lectisternium*). The accompanying banquet was restricted to senators, who shared in the feast by virtue of

---

[21] On the Saturnalia, see Beard, North, and Price 1998, 50, 80, 261 (vol. 1), 124–26 (vol. 2); Scullard 1981, 205–207. This celebration was also marked by temporary role reversal in which, for example, masters and slaves traded social roles. This inversion of social rank persisted in the post-classical world as well. See Stallybrass and White 1993, 284–92; Babcock 1978.

[22] On the Compitalia, see [Verg.] *Catal.* 13.27–30 (for text and commentary, see Westendorp Boerma 1963, 2:73–92). Augustus reorganized the festival in 7 B.C.E. as part of his program of religious restoration at Rome. See Beard, North, and Price 1998, 184–86 (vol. 1); also, Liebeschuetz 1979, 71.

[23] On the *Ludi Romani*, see Beard, North, and Price 1998, 40–41, 66–67 (vol. 1), 137–39 (vol. 2); Scullard 1981, 183–87; for the *Ludi Plebeii*, see Beard, North, and Price 1998, 40–41, 66–67 (vol. 1); Scullard 1981, 196–98.

having the "right of eating at public expense" (*ius publice epulandi*), a significant entitlement.[24]

A similar tendency to equate eating with political status is seen in the *Feriae Latinae*, a moveable feast in honor of Jupiter Latiaris, originally celebrated by the Latin League on the Alban Mount. Representatives from the forty-seven member cities took part in the festival and sacrifices over which the Romans exercised hegemony. According to our sources, each member city received one bull, which was to be sacrificed in common.[25] Additionally, each city brought different graded portions of food to the common feast while receiving differential portions of meat from the sacrificial bull. Furthermore, the more powerful cities received larger portions of meat than lesser members. A city that had shrunk to political insignificance could be denied a portion altogether.[26] Clearly, the *Feriae Latinae* featured both inclusion and hierarchical ordering, as it celebrated the political unity of the Latin League but also, through the careful controlling of food, the differences in rank among its members.

Exclusive dining marked two other well-known feasts, the *Ludi Megalenses* and *Ludi Cereales*. The *Ludi Megalenses*, held from 4 to 10 April to commemorate the arrival of the Magna Mater in Rome in 204 B.C.E., was noteworthy for the mutual exchange of hospitality and lavish meals (*mutitationes*) among patrician families.[27] On the other hand, the *Ludi Cereales* of 12 to 19 April, which celebrated the return of Persephone to earth, also included *mutitationes* (19 April), but they were available only to the plebs. The festal details remain sketchy, but we can suppose that the *Ludi Cereales* was clearly an opportunity for plebeians to enjoy their own exclusive feasts in the same way as did their patrician superiors earlier in the same month.[28]

---

[24] On the *ius publice epulandi*, see Suet. *Aug.* 35.

[25] Dion. Hal. 4.49.3.

[26] In general, see Scullard 1981, 111–15; Wissowa 1912, 35, 109–10; Latte 1960, 144–46; Lincoln 1985, 15–16.

[27] On *mutitationes*, see D'Arms 1984, 335–336 and n. 25. In general, see Beard, North, and Price 1998, 97, 102 (fig. 2.6 [d]), 138, 164 (vol. 1); 65, [Calendar from Praeneste], 68, [Calendar of Filocalus] (vol. 2); Scullard, 1981, 97–100.

[28] The *Ludi Cereales*, *Ludi Romani*, *Plebeii*, and *Ludi Megalenses* all survived at least into the mid-fourth century. See Salzman 1990, 120–30. We might also include in this category of restrictive public banqueting the Feast of the Ovens, or Fornacalia, a moveable, mid-winter celebration held not long after the Saturnalia. Although many of the details are obscure, it involved bread baking and feasting among the *curiae* of Rome, each of which had its own assembly hall. In this respect, the Fornacalia recalls the meals of the deme or phratry in Greek society. See Scullard 1981, 73; Latte 1960, 143.

Finally, public feasting in a ritual context cannot be entirely separated from drinking together in large numbers, especially since both activities were similar in their desire for camaraderie. At the feast of Anna Perenna on 15 March, plebeians celebrated the traditional Roman New Year by singing, drinking, and dancing near the Tiber. Here, men and women typically drank as many cups of wine as the number of years they prayed to live, a practice that surely must have led to the celebration getting out of hand from time to time.[29] The Parilia, similar to the Compitalia, began as a rural feast that likewise ended up in Rome, where it was especially known for drunken crowds jumping over heaps of burning hay. The meaning of this practice is not fully understood, but the inclusion of a large, open-air meal as part of the celebration remains at least a possibility among scholars, and at least one modern interpretation has argued for celebrations organized by the thirty *curiae* of the city.[30]

Two additional festivals have connections with group drinking, although there is less evidence for them than for the festivals mentioned above. The festival of Fors Fortuna, held on 24 June at the temple of Fortuna, was thought to appeal to plebeians and slaves, who drank upon flower-strewn riverboats. The Vinalia of 23 April may well have involved sampling of the previous year's wine harvest, thereby providing a ready-made opportunity for general feasting and drinking.[31]

In sum, the Roman religious calendar offered a rich diversity of commensal opportunities. Feasting or drinking occurred in the name of various divinities and at different places and times throughout the year. What is equally apparent is that, however much these festivals retained their religious character,[32] they placed an important emphasis on the sharing of food and/or drink. Furthermore, it is readily apparent that the Romans preferred to dine in distinct groups, whether priest, senator,

---

[29] See Ov. *Fast*. 3.523–32. The festival may also have been associated with sexual excess, perhaps indicated by Martial's characterization of Anna's grove as "delighting in virgin blood." See Sullivan 1991, 66, n. 25, and Harmon 1978, 1461, and n. 119.

[30] See Beard, North, and Price 1998, 174–76 (vol. 1), 116–19 (vol. 2); Scullard 1981, 103–105. On the possibility of a public meal, see Ogilvie 1970, 81–82.

[31] On the festival of Fors Fortuna, see Scullard 1981, 155–56. On the Vinalia, see Beard, North, and Price 1998, 45 (vol. 1) and designation on various calendars at 63–67 (vol. 2); Scullard, 1981, 106–108.

[32] On the religious nature of the sacrificial banquet throughout the Principate, see Scheid 1985, 193–206. For the traditional interpretation that these ceremonies became popularized (and hence, less religious) over time, see Daremberg and Saglio 1875–1919, s.v. "epula," 736–38.

plebeian, patrician, or *curia* member. Most notably, this feature of dining by groups persisted outside of religious festivals as well, as the evidence to follow will confirm.

SEGREGATIVE COMMENSALITY

The Meals of Roman Collegia

In sociological terms, segregative commensality is characterized as a means of setting up or restoring a group by limiting its membership to certain individuals through the act of sharing a meal. In some respects, this can often be a kind of therapy, a way for a group to gain self-identity, to keep tabs on its members, and even to confirm internal divisions or hierarchies. By its very nature, such an arrangement also strengthens the "We" against the "Not We," since the decision to invite some to a meal necessarily involves excluding others. The sharing of food contributes to this process by allowing for group exaltation, what we might commonly refer to as "blowing off some steam" or "dropping one's guard." Enhancing this feeling of euphoria is the satisfaction in knowing that others, i.e., the excluded, are "missing out" on something special.[33]

This kind of dining is most common in highly class-bound societies, the most striking example being modern India, where each caste is obligated to protect the purity of its food, even if this means that the members hide themselves while eating. Class-based societies, while less extreme than the caste-based model, also offer ample opportunities for restrictive eating, most apparent in the club-restaurant meals restricted to the upper elite of the central government, national research institutes, and corporations in France.[34] In America, too, we can observe this phenomenon in meals served at country clubs and social clubs, in which membership (and hence dining) is determined by wealth and status. We might even go so far as to include as less status-bound, but still segregative, the meals served in a college dining hall, especially in British universities or at most American faculty clubs and student dining halls, where faculty eat a more appetizing meal than the students.

When we turn to the ancient evidence, the segregative model would seem to fit especially well with those meals enjoyed by the many *collegia* of the Roman world. Comprised of free men and/or slaves and com-

---

[33] Grignon 2001, 28–29.
[34] Grignon 2001, 29–30.

monly centered around a specific deity or trade, the *collegium* met a strong desire for exclusivity in Roman society among the lower orders. Additionally, these clubs included their own benefactors (*patroni*) and administrative hierarchies, thereby allowing them to imitate in many ways the social and administrative organization of the larger society.[35]

To a great extent, the most distinguishing feature of these *collegia* was communal eating and drinking. A primary example is the *lex collegii* of the *cultores Dianae et Antinoi* from Lanuvium (C.E. 136), many of whose rules directly address banqueting on festal occasions. Here, we find that festal requirements are carefully detailed. For example, each supervising *magister* was required to provide "good wine," bread worth two *asses* for all the members, sardines, a single place setting, and warm water and utensils. Such specificity confirms the importance of the communal meal among groups of this sort.[36]

More revealing are the feasts associated with the college of Aesculapius and Hygia. The relevant text, dated to 153 C.E., records seven annual gatherings, a number that does not even include other likely feasts, such as those that celebrated the birthday of a patron or that were provided at a college's monthly business meeting (*conventus*).[37] Of the seven gatherings, five record food distributions for banquets. Among these were the bread, wine, and *sportulae* (presumably cash to purchase additional items) received by members on two funerary feast days, the *dies violaris* of 22 March and the *dies rosalis* of 11 May. The *Cara Cognatio*, the day of the family, or love feast, of 22 February, and the *natalis collegii* on 8 November also involved the distribution of bread, wine, and *sportulae*. Additionally, the *quinquennalis* (leader of the college) offered an annual *cena* to the membership, although it seems that a *sportula* could be substituted instead.[38] Most striking in this evidence is the importance of

---

[35] For the political nature of Roman *collegia*, see Cotter 1996, 74–89. The slaves of the emperor and of private households also formed *collegia*. See, e.g., *CIL* 6.10237.

[36] *CIL* 14.2112 = *ILS* 7212; Waltzing 1895–1900, 3.642–46. For a complete translation in English (reduced to extracts in the third edition, 1990), see Lewis and Reinhold 1966, 2.273–75.

[37] *CIL* 6.10234 = *ILS* 7213; Waltzing 1895–1900, 3.268–71; Gordon 1958–65, 2.90–94, n. 217; Gordon 1983, 148–50, with text also in Appendix 2.

[38] In chronological order, the feasts included: (1) 8 January: *strenae*; (2) 22 February (*Cara Cognatio*): *sportulae, panis, vinum*; (3) 14 March: *cena* furnished by *quinquennalis* Ofilius Hermes; (4) 22 March (*dies violaris*): *sportulae, panis, vinum*; (5) 11 May (*dies rosalis*): *sportulae, panis, vinum*; (6) 19 September (*dies natalis Antonini Pii*): *sportulae*; and (7) 8 November (*natalis collegii*): *sportulae, panis, vinum*.

rank in determining the amount of food and money received by each of the college's sixty members. Typically, the *quinquennalis*, along with the patrons, received the largest amount of food or money. Next came the dues-exempt members (*immunes*) and then the *curatores*. Rank-and-file members (*populi*) received the smallest shares.

Elsewhere, the evidence is quite similar: seven annual feasts for the ebony and ivory workers; three for the fishermen and workers of the bed and banks of the Tiber; five for the college of Silvanus at Lucania; six for the funerary college of Diana and Antinous at Lanuvium.[39] In all these instances, we can suppose that the administrative procedures were similar, as was the simple desire for fellowship and escape from the tedium of daily life through the sharing of food and drink.

Given this mindset, these gatherings sometimes breached the boundaries of decorum, a reality evident in the punishments recorded for bad behavior among the festal celebrants.[40] More importantly, these banquets provided a setting not only for social interaction but also for creating hierarchies that could not be found outside of the *collegium*. Only in this context, for example, could a common cult worshipper become a leader and confirm his status through his access to the largest amount of food and drink. As this type of evidence suggests, food played an undeniable role in shaping and reinforcing Roman attitudes toward rank and status. As both a perishable good and critical commodity, food was readily open to control and manipulation of all sorts. In this respect, it was both a unique and highly effective substance whose potential for purposes beyond the simply nutritive was well understood by the Romans.

TRANSGRESSIVE COMMENSALITY

The Cenae *of Domitian*

The final category to consider is transgressive commensality. Characterized by Grignon as the opposition between social groups and the borders that separate them, this type of feasting both recognizes these borders and allows them to be crossed temporarily in order to provide a relationship of exchange between parties of different social or economic status.

---

[39] On the ebony and ivory workers, see *CIL* 6.33885; on fishermen and divers of the Tiber, see *CIL* 6.1872; on Silvanus, see *CIL* 10.444; on Diana and Antinous, see *CIL* 14.2112.

[40] For ancient criticism of this type of behavior, see Philo, *Spec. Leg.* 2.145–46.

It is precisely by crossing such borders that transgressive commensality maintains them.[41] Extreme examples of this form of dining are typical of hierarchical societies. They might include the "invitation au chateau" (invitation to the manor) or a politician lunching with workers at the factory. In modern sociological terms, three features are common to this activity: (1) the asymmetry of the relationship between the superior and the inferior diners; (2) the need for the dominant host to be recognizable among his guests, offering himself in the process as a "gift" to the diners for a certain period of time; and (3) the requirement that the dominant party eat the same food as everybody else in order to show that he recognizes common needs and tastes.[42]

Given these features, this type of commensality is especially characteristic of monarchical societies, where the social and political gulf between ruler and subjects is vast. The most extreme and ultimately tragic example of this reality was the coronation banquet of Nicholas and Alexandra in nineteenth-century imperial Russia, where the royal couple dined extravagantly among their seven thousand guests but were well removed from them. The populace, prohibited from entering the palace, was entitled to drafts of beer at a military training field, only to die by the thousands in a stampede that followed rumors of diminishing supplies.[43]

In a Roman context, transgressive commensality finds its fullest expression in the imperially sponsored formal dinner, the *cena*.[44] Especially favored by Domitian in the later first century, the *cena* is praised by the likes of the court poet Statius for its lavish food, social mix of diners, and the active presence of the emperor himself. Quite rightly, Statius' exuberance about Domitianic court life has attracted its share of scholarly skepticism.[45] Nevertheless, it is worthwhile to examine this meal in light of Grignon's criteria for what it can tell us about transgressive commensality among the Romans and the nature of social interaction on such occasions.

In the first place, Domitian's feasts illuminate quite dramatically Grignon's first feature of transgressive commensality, which calls for an

[41] See Grignon 2001, 30–31.
[42] Grignon 2001, 31.
[43] For an account of this tragedy, see Massie 1967, 56–57.
[44] The meal is sometimes referred to as a *cena recta*, a term whose origin and meaning are not entirely clear. See D'Arms 1990, 309.
[45] See Stat. *Silv.* 1.6.43–50; on scholarly skepticism, see D'Arms 1990, 310, and Millar 1992, 79.

asymmetrical relationship between the host and his guests. In the first place, by the later first century C.E., emperors' feasts were nothing new. As with so many things, they had begun with Augustus, with the ancient sources tending to equate the tone and tenor of such feasts with the character and personality of the emperor who sponsored them. In this setting, social distancing was inevitable. Nevertheless, this aspect was especially pronounced under Domitian, who not only preferred to be addressed as *Dominus et Deus* ("Master and God"), but also arranged the dining room (*triclinium*) of the *Domus Flavia* with an eye towards underscoring the realities of social asymmetry. This latter feature is most apparent in the disposition of the flat apse of the dining room's end wall, where the emperor himself either sat or reclined on a *triclinium*, well removed from but still in full sight of his hundreds of guests. By using the apse in this way, that is, by personalizing it with his presence, Domitian ensured that his feasts took on the character of a theatrical performance in which his guests became both spectators and participants at the same time.[46]

This arrangement dramatically emphasized the distance between the emperor and his guests, both in physical and social terms. The grandeur of the *triclinium* itself surely enhanced this reality.[47] At the same time, by positioning himself in this way, Domitian became immediately recognizable among his guests, thereby fulfilling Grignon's second feature of transgressive commensality as mentioned above. It seems then that already by the later first century C.E., the process that would eventually lead to the complete sequestering of the monarch at table had taken root in the shimmering opulence of the Palatine palace.

Finally, while the *cenae* of Domitian seem to fulfill Grignon's first two criteria for transgressive commensality, the ancient evidence is much less clear on Grignon's third requirement that all in attendance eat the same food. On the one hand, the ancient sources praise Domitian for inviting all orders of Roman society to eat the same fare at the same

---

[46] Bek 1983, 90–94.

[47] Statius claimed that the room was "more spacious than an open field" (*Silv.* 4.2.23–24) and allowed guests "to recline together at 1,000 tables" (*Silv.* 4.2.32–33). The height of the dining room itself was also spectacular, with Statius proclaiming that the dome of the palace was so expansive that it appeared to cover a large part of the sky. On this latter aspect, see Coleman (1988) at *Silvae* 4.2, l.24 (*operti*). Similarly, Martial proclaims the *triclinium* as a place worthy of the gods; see 7.56, 8.36. A recent treatment of the *triclinium*, suggesting the presence of a timber roof 33 meters high, lends perspective to these poetic depictions. See Gibson, DeLaine, and Claridge 1994, 77–87.

table.[48] In fact, based on evidence from elsewhere in the Roman world, it would seem that the social distancing present on these occasions was reinforced by the differences, not the similarities, in festal fare. We witness this most clearly in a feast offered by Domitian on one occasion in the Flavian Amphitheatre, where the upper classes received higher quality fare than the *populus*. Furthermore, Martial confirms this same custom among *cenae* sponsored by wealthy private Romans in which, as a humble *cliens*, he was denied the oysters, mushrooms, turbot, and turtle doves that his social superiors enjoyed.[49] Additionally, similar social distinctions were a part of provincial dining practices as well, as evident in the differences in meals based on rank at various statue dedications and public events in the Roman West.[50]

Much as we witnessed earlier in the instance of *collegia*, the picture at the emperor's table, then, is one of social differentiation reinforced by the manipulation of food. On the other hand, even if the fare differed on these occasions, it did not seem to dim the appeal of banqueting with one's superiors. On the contrary, Suetonius' mention of a wealthy provincial, who once offered 200,000 sesterces for the chance to dine with the emperor Caligula, vividly underscores the value attached to such a meal in the socially competitive world of first-century Rome.[51]

[48] The relevant passages read as follows: *una vescitur omnis ordo mensa, parvi, femina, plebs, eques, senatus: libertas reverentiam remisit . . .* "Every class eats at one table, children, woman, plebeian, knight, senate: freedom has relaxed the sense of reverence . . ." (Stat. *Silv.* 1.6.43–45); *iam se, quisquis is est, inops, beatus, convivam ducis esse gloriatur.* "Now, whoever he is, poor, rich, boasts himself a dinner guest of the emperor" (1.6.49–50).

[49] On Domitian's feast at the Colosseum, see Statius's reference to the "more luxurious fare" delivered by handsome attendants (*Silv.* 1.6.28–34), surely an indication of the food designated for elites. Social distinctions were further underscored, of course, by separate seating sections by class within such venues. See Claridge 1998, 276–83; also, Richardson 1992, s.v. "Amphitheatrum Flavium," 48; Kolendo 1981, 301–15. Similar distinctions prevailed at other entertainments in the Colosseum as well. See Coleman 1990, 44–73. For Martial and inferior fare, see 3.60. Here we have to wonder too, based on the first line of the epigram (*non iam venalis ut ante . . .* "I am no longer on the payroll") if perhaps the poet is someone else's client now, and therefore even less deserving of high-quality food.

[50] See the decurions and their sons at Iuvanum (*CIL* 9.2962) receiving a *cena* while the *plebs* are offered an *epulum*; or at Spoletium (*CIL* 11.4815 = *ILS* 6638), where a bequest of 250,000 sesterces provided an annual public *cena* for the decurions (*in publico cenarent*); other groups on the same occasion were invited only "to eat in public" (*in publico vescerentur*).

[51] Suet. *Cal.* 39.

CONCLUSION

Commensality, by definition, is based on the collectivist consumption of goods exclusively reserved for members of a group. The typologies examined in this paper help us to categorize this particular brand of collectivist behavior in a manner that confirms its universality while compelling us to look more carefully at some of its most prominent features in a Roman context. To sum up, two points are worth emphasizing.

First, the Romans' or any other festal peoples' behavior tends to confirm the modern sociological observation that recognizes in festal activity the need of establishing and maintaining group identity—in short, of "fitting in."[52] In the Roman world, this played itself out on any number of public occasions and on several levels—between emperor and his subjects, municipal benefactor and his beneficiaries, or the *quinquennalis* of a *collegium* and his fellow members. This impulse is especially characteristic of hierarchical societies. It should come as no surprise, therefore, that the impulse to "fit in" found ready acceptance not only in Rome but throughout the municipalities of the West, which were eager to reduplicate on the local level all that the imperial city had to offer.

Second, it is not so surprising that food played such a prominent role in this social process, given that it simultaneously allows for communal participation and social separation. The Romans recognized this aspect as readily as any other culture, ancient or modern. Thus, they were able to incorporate large-scale feasting among a broad array of collectivist activities that helped to define what it meant to be truly Roman, or more specifically perhaps, what it meant to be truly Roman within the rigid class structure of ancient society.[53]

THE COLLEGE OF WILLIAM & MARY
e-mail: jfdona@wm.edu

BIBLIOGRAPHY

Aldrete, G. S., and D. J. Mattingly. 1999. "Feeding the City: The Organization, Operation, and Scale of the Supply System for Rome." In *Life, Death, and Entertainment in the Roman Empire*, ed. D. S. Potter and D. J. Mattingly, 171–204. Michigan: University of Michigan Press.

[52] Grignon 2001, 31.
[53] I wish to thank the editor and anonymous readers for their very helpful comments and suggestions. Any errors, of course, remain my own.

Babcock, Barbara, ed. 1978. *The Reversible World: Symbolic Inversion in Art and Society*. Ithaca: Cornell University Press.

Beard, Mary. 1985. "Writing and Ritual: A Study of Diversity and Expansion in the *Arval Acta*." *PBSR* 53:114–62.

Beard, Mary, John North, and Simon Price. 1998. *Religions of Rome*. 2 vols. Cambridge: Cambridge University Press.

Bek, Lise. 1983. "*Questiones Convivales*: The Idea of the *Triclinium* and the Staging of Convivial Ceremony from Rome to Byzantium." *ARID* 12:81–107.

Bowie, A. M. 1995. "Greek Sacrifice: Forms and Functions." In *The Greek World*, ed. Anton Powell, 463–82. London: Routledge.

Burke, Peter. 1978. *Popular Culture in Early Modern Europe*. New York: New York University Press.

Claridge, Amanda. 1998. *Rome: An Oxford Archaeological Guide*. Oxford: Oxford University Press.

Coleman, Kathleen, ed. and comm. 1988. *Statius: Silvae IV*. Oxford: Oxford University Press.

———. 1990. "Fatal Charades: Roman Executions Staged as Mythological Enactments." *JRS* 80:44–73.

Cotter, Wendy. 1996. "The *Collegia* and Roman Law: State Restrictions on Voluntary Associations, 64 B.C.E.–299 C.E." In *Voluntary Associations in the Graeco-Roman World*, ed. J. S. Kloppenborg and S. G. Wilson, 74–89. London: Routledge.

Cressy, David. 1997. *Birth, Marriage, and Death: Ritual, Religion, and the Life-Cycle in Tudor and Stuart England*. Oxford: Oxford University Press.

Daremberg, Charles, and Edmond Saglio. 1875–1919, 5 vols. *Dictionnaire des antiquités grecques et romaines*. Paris: Librarie Hachette.

D'Arms, John. 1984. "Control, Companionship, and *Clientela*: Some Social Functions of the Roman Communal Meal." *EMC* 28:327–48.

———. 1990. "The Roman *Convivium* and the Idea of Equality." In *Sympotica: A Symposium on the Symposion*, ed. Oswyn Murray, 308–20. Oxford: Oxford University Press.

Donahue, John. 2004, forthcoming. *The Roman Community at Table during the Principate*. Michigan: University of Michigan Press.

Dumézil, Georges. 1975. *Fêtes romaines d'été et d'automne suivi de dix questions romaines*. Paris: Gallimard.

Dupont, Florence. 1999. "The Grammar of Roman Dining." In *Food: A Culinary History*, ed. Flandrin and Montanari, 113–27.

Dunbabin, K. M. D. 1993. "Wine and Water at the Roman *Convivium*." *JRA* 6:116–41.

———. 1999. *Mosaics of the Greek and Roman World*. Cambridge: Cambridge University Press.

Farb, Peter, and George Armelagos. 1980. *Consuming Passions: The Anthropology of Eating*. Boston: Houghton Mifflin.

Flandrin, Jean-Louis, and Massimo Montanari. 1999. *Food: A Culinary History from Antiquity to the Present*. New York: Columbia University Press.

Garnsey, Peter. 1968. "Trajan's *Alimenta*: Some Problems." *Historia* 17:367–81.

———. 1988. *Famine and Food Supply: Responses to Risk and Crisis*. Cambridge: Cambridge University Press.

———. 1990. "Responses to Food Crisis in the Ancient Mediterranean World." In *Hunger in History: Food Shortage, Poverty, and Deprivation*, ed. L. F. Newman, 126–46. Oxford: Oxford University Press.

Gibson, Sheila, J. DeLaine, and Amanda Claridge. 1994. "The *Triclinium* of the *Domus Flavia*: A New Reconstruction." *PBSR* 62:67–100.

Gordon, A. E. 1958–65. *Album of Dated Latin Inscriptions*. Berkeley and Los Angeles: University of California Press.

———. 1983. *Illustrated Introduction to Latin Epigraphy*. 4 vols. Berkeley and Los Angeles: University of California Press.

Gowers, Emily. 1993. *The Loaded Table: Representations of Food in Roman Literature*. Oxford: Oxford University Press.

Grignon, Claude. 2001. "Commensality and Social Morphology: An Essay of Typology." In *Food, Drink, and Identity: Cooking, Eating, and Drinking in Europe since the Middle Ages*, ed. Peter Scholliers, 23–33. Oxford: Oxford University Press.

Harmon, D. P. 1978. "The Public Festivals of Rome." *ANRW* 2.16.2:1440–68.

Hudson, Nicola. 1993. "The Beast at the Feast: Food in Roman Verse Satire." *Food, Culture & History* 1:204–19.

Kajava, Mika. 1998. "Visceratio." *Arctos* 32:109–31.

Kolendo, Jerzy. 1981. "La répartition des places aux spectacles et la stratification sociale dans l'Empire romain." *Ktèma* 6:301–15.

Latte, Kurt. 1960. *Römische Religionsgeschichte*. Munich: C. H. Beck.

Lewis, Naphtali, and Meyer Reinhold, eds. 1966. *Roman Civilization*. 2 vols. New York: Harper.

Liebeschuetz, J. H. W. G. 1979. *Continuity and Change in Roman Religion*. Oxford: Oxford University Press.

Lincoln, Bruce. 1985. "Of Meat and Society, Sacrifice and Creation, Butchers and Philosophy." *L'Uomo* 9:9–29.

Massie, Robert. 1967. *Nicholas and Alexandra*. New York: Atheneum.

Millar, Fergus. 1992. *The Emperor in the Roman World, 31 B.C.–A.D. 337*. Ithaca: Cornell University Press.

Mrozek, Stanislaw. 1987. *Les distributions d'argent et de nourriture dans les villes italiennes du Haut-Empire romain*. Brussels: Latomus.

Myerhoff, Barbara. 1982. "Rites of Passage: Process and Paradox." In *Celebration: Studies in Festivity and Ritual*, ed. Victor Turner, 109–35. Washington, D.C.: Smithsonian Institution Press.

Ogilvie, R. M. 1970. *The Romans and Their Gods in the Age of Augustus*. New York: Norton.

Pudliszewski, Jacek. 1992. "L' *epulum* dans les inscriptions espagnoles." *Eos* 80:69–76.

Richardson, L. R., Jr. 1992. *A New Topographical Dictionary of Ancient Rome.* Baltimore: Johns Hopkins University Press.

Riggsby, A. M. 1997. " 'Public' and 'Private' in Roman Culture: The Case of the *Cubiculum.*" *JRA* 10:36–56.

Salzman, M. R. 1990. *On Roman Time: The Codex-Calendar of 354 and the Rhythms of Urban Life in Late Antiquity.* Berkeley and Los Angeles: University of California Press.

Scheid, John. 1985. "Sacrifice et banquet à Rome: Quelques problèmes." *MEFRA* 97:193–206.

———. 1990a. *Le collège des Frères Arvales: Étude prosopographique du recrutement, 69-304.* Rome: "L' Erma" di Bretschneider.

———. 1990b. *Romulus et ses frères: le Collège des Frères Arvales, modèle du culte public dans la Rome des empereurs.* Rome: École française de Rome.

Schmitt-Pantel, Pauline. 1992. *La cité au banquet: Histoire des repas publics dans les cités   grecques.* Rome: École française de Rome.

Scullard, H. H. 1981. *Festivals and Ceremonies of the Roman Republic.* New York: Cornell University Press.

Slater, William, ed. 1991. *Dining in a Classical Context.* Michigan: University of Michigan Press.

———. 2000. "Handouts at Dinner." *Phoenix* 54:107–22.

Stallybrass, Peter, and A. White. 1993. "Bourgeois Hysteria and the Carnivalesque." In *The Cultural Studies Reader,* ed. Simon During, 284–92. London: Routledge.

Sullivan, J. P. 1991. *Martial, the Unexpected Classic: A Literary and Historical Study.* Cambridge: Cambridge University Press.

Syme, Ronald. 1980. *Some Arval Brethren.* Oxford: Oxford University Press.

Taylor, L. R. 1942. "Caesar's Colleagues in the Pontifical College." *AJP* 63:385–412.

van Berchem, Denis. 1975. *Les distributions de blé et d'argent à la plèbe romaine sous l'empire.* New York: Arno Press.

Wallace-Hadrill, Andrew 1994. *Houses and Society in Pompeii and Herculaneum.* Princeton: Princeton University Press.

Waltzing, J.-P. 1895–1900. *Étude historique sur les corporations professionnelles.* 4 vols. Louvain: C. Peeters.

Wesch-Klein, Gabriele. 1993. *Funus publicum: eine Studie zur öffentlichen Beisetzung und Gewährung von Ehrengräbern in Rom und den West-provinzen.* Stuttgart: F. Steiner.

Westendorp Boerma, R. E. H., ed. and comm. 1949–63. *P. Vergili Maronis libellum qui inscribitur Catalepton.* 2 vols. Assen: De Torenlaan.

Wissowa, Georg. 1912. *Religion und Kultus der Römer.* Munich: C. H. Beck.

Illustrations

Figures a–d (Roller)

Figures 1–25 (Dunbabin)

Fig. a. After Altmann 1905, 153, fig. 124

Fig. b. Photo Rossa, Deutsches Archäologisches Institut, neg. no. 74.727

Fig. c. After Altmann 1905, 192, fig. 154

Fig. d. After Herrmann-Bruckmann 1904, Taf. 210.

Fig. 1. Rome, House on Caelian, wall painting of servant with plate of vegetables. Naples, Museo Nazionale Inv. 84285. DAI(R) 75.1467, photo Rossa.

Fig. 2. Rome, House on Caelian, upper half of servant with plate of food. Naples, Museo Nazionale Inv. 84286. DAI(R) 75.1470, photo Rossa.

Fig. 3. Rome, House on Caelian, wine-server. Naples, Museo Nazionale Inv. 84284. DAI(R) 75.1466, photo Rossa.

Fig. 4. Rome, Schola Praeconum, wall painting of servants. DAI(R) 76.2356, photo Rossa.

Fig. 5. Carthage, mosaic of preparations for banquet. Paris, Musée du Louvre Ma
1795. After *Inv. Tun.* 764.

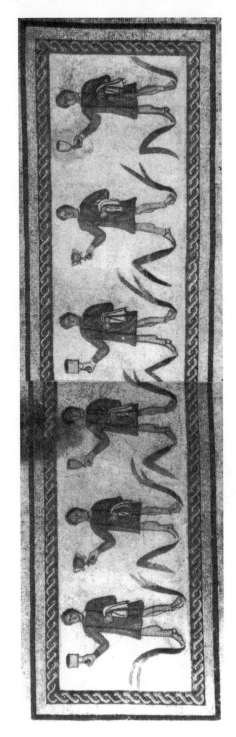

Fig. 6. Complutum, House of Bacchus, mosaic of servants. Photo courtesy D. Fernández Galiano.

Fig. 7. Uthina, mosaic threshold from House of Fructus. Tunis, Musée du Bardo A 137. Photo KMDD.

Fig. 8. Ephesos, House by Odeion, wall painting of servant with plate of figs.
Photo courtesy V. M. Strocka.

Fig. 9. Ephesos, House by Odeion, wall painting of servant with glass and towel. Photo courtesy V. M. Strocka.

Fig. 10. Ephesos, House by Odeion, wall painting of reclining *dominus*.
Photo courtesy V. M. Strocka.

Fig. 11. Rome, sarcophagus of Caecilius Vallianus, Vatican, Museo Gregoriano Profano. Inv. 9538/9539. DAI(R) 90.413, photo Anger.

On the sarcophagus, the inscription reads:

D   S
P·CAECILI
VALLIANI
A·M·LITIS
VIXIT·ANN

Fig. 12. Sarcophagus
fragment from
Rome, Staatliche
Museen zu Berlin—
Preussischer
Kulturbesitz,
Skulpturensammlung
und Museum für
Byzantinische Kunst,
Inv. 2786. Photo
courtesy Museum.

Fig. 13. Rome, sarcophagus fragment, Palazzo Mattei. DAI(R) 29.417, photo Fraglia.

Fig. 14. Rome, fragmentary sarcophagus lid, Museo Nazionale Romano. DAI(R) 72.538, photo Singer.

Fig. 15. Rome, Catacomb of Peter and Marcellinus, *cubiculum* 10, servants on entrance wall. After Wilpert 1903, pl. 107.3.

Fig. 16. Viminacium, drawing of tomb paintings. After Valeva 2001, fig. 36, courtesy J. Valeva.

Fig. 17. Capua, Museo Campano, mosaic of *paedagogium*. DAI(R) 64.660, photo Hutzel.

Fig. 18. Pompeii, Casa dei Vettii (VI 15.1), atrium c, painting of child holding jug and basin. Photo DAI(R) 31.1781.

Fig. 19. Esquiline Treasure, Casket of Projecta, front, toilet of Projecta on body, marine Venus on lid. London, British Museum, Department of Medieval and Later Antiquities 1866.12-29.1. Copyright © The British Museum.

Fig. 20. Esquiline Treasure, Casket of Projecta, left end, procession of servants. London, British Museum, Department of Medieval and Later Antiquities 1866.12-29.1. Copyright © The British Museum.

Fig. 21. Esquiline Treasure, Casket of Projecta, back panel of lid, procession to baths. London, British Museum, Department of Medieval and Later Antiquities 1866.12-29.1. Copyright © The British Museum.

Fig. 22. Piazza Armerina, vestibule to baths, mosaic of lady and servants entering baths. Fototeca Unione.

Fig. 23. Silistra (Durostorum), tomb, general view. DAI(R) 86.164, photo Tschiligirov.

Fig. 24. Silistra, tomb, female servant holding jug and basin. DAI(R) 86.183, photo Tschiligirov.

Fig. 25. Silistra, tomb, young male servant holding up cloak. DAI(R) 86.185, photo Tschiligirov.

THE WAITING SERVANT IN LATER ROMAN ART

KATHERINE M. D. DUNBABIN

Abstract. Although literary sources from the early Empire attest to the importance attached to the presence of a large staff of specialized servants at the banquets of the wealthy, in the art of this period little emphasis is placed upon the servants in banquet scenes, who serve essentially utilitarian functions. By the later Empire, however, figures of attendants bearing offerings become much more prominent and convey messages of the wealth and status of the owners and of the lavishness of their hospitality. The article studies the iconographical sources of these figures and compares the processions of servants shown in other contexts as part of the general representation of the life of luxury.

I

IN A MEMORABLE PAPER delivered at the second symposium on Symposia in 1989 (published as *Dining in a Classical Context*), John D'Arms made us turn our eyes away from the upper-class participants in Roman banquets and consider instead the plight of the "human props" required to maintain them, the slaves.[1] Citing literary sources predominantly of the early Empire, occasionally complemented by inscriptions, he painted a vivid picture of the vast throngs of servants needed to run the banquets of wealthy Romans, of their varied and specialized tasks, and of the demeanour and characteristics expected of them, as well as of the treatment, good or bad, meted out to them by their masters. The sources make it clear that the presence of such crowds of attendants, the *mancipiorum legiones* of Pliny, was not only essential for the practical administration of the banquet, but was a major contributor to the prestige and status of

---

[1] D'Arms 1991, 171. I have preferred the terms "servants" or "attendants" to "slaves" in this article, as the function of the figures represented in the works discussed is of greater significance than their legal status.

Illustrations appear in a gallery following page 114

the hosts, who prided themselves both upon the numbers of such attendants that they could provide and upon their elegance and skills. Moralists and satirists stress the value placed by the rich and fashionable upon the physical beauty of their table servants, the elegance of their dress, hair-styles, and deportment, and the skill and accomplishment with which they performed their tasks.[2] They were no less essential for the successful achievement of even a small dinner than the variety of the food served, the fineness of the wines, and the elaborateness and richness of the drinking and serving vessels. For the guests, as Juvenal satirically makes clear, it was an important marker of status whether one's wine was served by an elegant young boy or by a more proletarian household slave, as central to distinctions as the quality of the wine itself.[3]

A passage from one of Seneca's letters shows with exceptional clarity the effect that might be desired. He writes of the "most arrogant custom that surrounds the master as he dines with a crowd of standing slaves" and goes on to speak of the silence enforced on these slaves, in which not only speech but an accidental cough or sneeze was punished by flogging; the whole night they must stand hungry and dumb.[4] Reclining to dine was, always, a position conveying power and status in the ancient world; it is easy to imagine how this effect might be enhanced by the presence of the standing, silent attendants.[5] In another letter Seneca writes of the "flocks of unfortunate boys" and the serried ranks of elegant pages (*exoleti*), drawn up according to their nationality and colour, their type of hair, or the degree of first down on their cheeks.[6] Seneca writes of course with moralising intent: the first passage quoted comes from his letter urging the humane treatment of one's slaves, the second from an attack upon the luxury of his fellow aristocrats. His arguments

[2] Plin. *NH* 33.26; for other sources see D'Arms 1991, and below nn. 41–44.

[3] Juv. 5.52–66.

[4] Sen. *Ep.* 47. 2–3: "itaque rideo istos qui turpe existimant cum servo suo cenare: quare, nisi quia superbissima consuetudo cenanti domino stantium servorum turbam circumdedit? . . . nocte tota ieiuni mutique perstant." Contrast the practice of Galba in distributing his leftovers to the servants standing *ad pedes*, a custom that provokes Suetonius' disapproving comments: Suet. *Galba* 22, and cf. Petr. *Sat.* 64.13, 67.1 (I owe these references to an anonymous reviewer for *AJP*).

[5] A similar contrast (though eliciting a different response) lies behind Juv. 5.65: the beautiful wine server is indignant at being ask to serve an old client, *quodque aliquid poscas et quod se stante recumbas*.

[6] Sen. *Ep.* 95. 24: "transeo puerorum infelicium greges...transeo agmina exoletorum per nationes coloresque discripta ut eadem omnibus levitas sit, eadem primae mensura lanuginis, eadem species capillorum . . ." For the importance of hair, see below n. 44.

may therefore contain much that is conventional, with details exaggerated or invented for moralistic effect; nevertheless, the images he presents must have been recognizable and familiar to his readers.[7]

One might expect, therefore, that the possession of such fine servants, and in large numbers, would be advertised visually by their owners or be emulated in art even by those who could themselves not boast of sufficient wealth. Yet, as D'Arms acknowledged in his paper, the scenes of the banquet represented in Roman art of the early Empire hardly bear this out.[8] Servants, both male and female, duly appear in attendance upon the reclining guests; but for the most part they are unobtrusive. One or two are usually included, represented on a smaller scale than the guests; this use of hierarchical scale both indicates their lesser importance and the fact that they are intended to be understood as youthful. They serve essential functional purposes, most often pouring the wine or bringing a cup to their masters; a few perform less stereotyped services, such as supporting a drunken guest.[9] The antecedents of course go back to banquet scenes in Greek art, which from the late archaic period onwards almost always include the *pais* to serve the wine; in Attic vase-painting and votive reliefs he is usually shown as a beautiful nude boy.[10] In some of the so-called Totenmahl reliefs, funerary reliefs of the late classical and early Hellenistic periods showing the deceased at the banquet, a tendency appears to increase the numbers of such servants, who are now often shown clothed.[11] The aim is clearly to enhance the honorific value of the scene by laying greater stress upon the wealth and status of the deceased. But the servants remain a minor feature; it was evidently felt undesirable to multiply the numbers of attendants in banquet scenes or to stress their role and significance to the point where they might come to predominate over the figures of the diners themselves.

---

[7] On the other side of the coin, another passage of Seneca (*Constant.* 11.3) shows slaves encouraged to engage in repartee at the dinner table and even to insult their masters and the guests for amusement: see Peachin 2001, 137. Clearly, practice could vary widely depending on the taste and mood of the host, and neither aspect should be accepted uncritically as the norm. My concern here, however, is with the ideologies expressed and their expression in art, rather than with trying to establish what was "normal" behaviour at any hypothetical Roman dinner party.

[8] D'Arms 1991, 178.

[9] See, for example, the servants in the three paintings of banquets from the Casa del Triclinio in Pompeii (V 2.4): Fröhlich 1991, 222–29, pls. 20.2–21. Further examples in Dunbabin 2003, chap. 2.

[10] Cf. Schäfer 1997, 61–64; Dentzer 1982, 322–25; more generally, Himmelmann 1971.

[11] Fabricius 1999, 92–94, 117–18, 230–32.

If, on the other hand, we turn to the art of the third and fourth centuries C.E., we find a substantial number of representations, in painting, mosaic, and sculpture, which illustrate perfectly Seneca's image of the crowd of standing slaves. Among the finest are a series of paintings from a building on the Caelian Hill in Rome, to be dated in the first half of the fourth century.[12] An engraving from 1783 showing the excavations in progress reveals the original system of decoration, with the individual figures framed in panels, separated by candelabra, and surrounded by garlands.[13] Two and a half figures, about two-thirds lifesize, survive today (in the Museo Nazionale in Naples); the rest are known from the eighteenth-century engravings (figs. 1–3). Six of them showed servants hurrying forward, carrying big plates laden with food, which ranges from a suckling pig and a chicken to a variety of fruits and vegetables, with a dish for the sauce. All the servants wear sleeved calf-length tunics, richly adorned with embroidered *orbiculi* on the shoulders. Two have long flowing curls; the rest are short-haired. The seventh figure is the wine server, holding up a cup or glass in one hand and with a sieve hanging from one finger of the other. Two tall flasks in a wicker case stand on the ground beside him. He is even more richly dressed, his tunic adorned with *clavi* embroidered with purple and gold as well as *orbiculi* on his shoulder and at the hem; his hair is long and curly.[14] It is not clear from the surviving evidence whether the lost portion of the room might have contained other figures, such as the *dominus* and *domina* ready to receive the servants' offerings. But isolated in their panels as the servants stand, they do not need to be associated with any further scene; their offerings may be directed to the actual occupants of the room.

That certainly is how the paintings of another Roman monument, the Schola Praeconum, should be read. A building of the Severan period on the southwest slopes of the Palatine, facing onto the Circus Maximus, has been identified as the headquarters of the public heralds, the *praecones*, and perhaps of other minor public officials.[15] One of the three rooms

---

[12] Donati 1998, 292, nos. 67–69. Santa Maria Scrinari 1991, 50–52, 142, suggests that the building may have formed part of the Imperial Palace on the Lateran; but see Liverani 1988, who identifies it rather as a rich private house.

[13] Engraving reproduced in Mielsch 1978, 167–68, pl. 86.2.

[14] Mielsch 1978, pls. 87, 88.1; Baratte 1990, 92–95, figs. 1–6. For the sieve, see M. Martin in Cahn and Kaufmann-Heinimann 1984, 112, pl. 32.

[15] Marchetti 1892, 44–48; Papi 1999, 254–55; Bollmann 1998, 261–65, A18. The specific identification is based upon the mosaic showing men carrying *vexilla* and *caducei*, which was inserted into the room with the paintings in a subsequent (fourth century?) phase; the position of the building and its proximity to the Paedagogium make it likely that it always had some similar function.

opening off the courtyard was decorated (in a second phase, perhaps in the mid third century) with wall paintings showing approximately lifesize male figures against an architectural background; seven of the original eight survive (fig. 4).[16] They wear sleeved, knee-length tunics, white with two narrow *clavi*. On the left-hand wall, next to the entrance, one man advances as though to greet those entering, staff in one hand, the other outstretched. Three more stand at intervals further along the wall: one holding a towel or napkin, one a garland, the third apparently a box. The three figures on the opposite, right-hand wall are more damaged but include one with garland, one with napkin, and the legs of a third with a pair of sandals beside him. Objects lying on the ground beside these figures include what seem to be a flywhisk and a box for perfumes. The servants either advance as though to greet those entering or stand frontally to face into the room; all their action is directed out of the painting and into the real space of the room. There is no representation of a banquet scene, nor any painted guests; the viewer must take the objects held by the servants, and their assiduous actions, as directed towards those participating in real banquets in the room itself.

Outside Rome, the same theme is found on mosaics and paintings. A fine mosaic from Carthage shows a series of figures moving against a plain white ground; one survives complete, four others in part (fig. 5).[17] The complete figure is a young man whose tunic is tied in a knot at his loins; he carries a flat basket apparently containing loaves. A smaller figure, presumably a young boy, holds a smaller basket, perhaps with flowers; another, with a scarf or towel around his shoulders, holds a long-necked flask and perhaps a basin. Another, of whom only one arm and a leg survive, holds by the handle an elaborate bronze cauldron that can be recognized as a hot-water heater, an *authepsa*.[18] Finally, the upper half of a powerful man, wearing only a tunic over one shoulder, holds one end of a pole; he is evidently one of a pair carrying a heavy object. Although earlier commentators identified the scene as showing the preparations for a religious ceremony, there seems no reason to see it as anything

---

[16] Cagiano de Azevedo 1947–1949, 253–58, proposing a date ca. 200–240 for the paintings. This has been generally accepted, but see Mielsch 2001, 121–22, who places them later in the late third or early fourth century.

[17] Dunbabin 1978, 124, 142, pl. 115; Baratte 1978, 71–74, no. 36. In my 1978 book, I proposed a date for the mosaic in the late second or early third century, but I would now prefer to place it substantially later in the third century; however, Baratte (loc. cit.) suggests ca. 180–190. I also no longer believe, as I was inclined to do then, that there is any reason to connect it with a cult banquet of any sort.

[18] For the *authepsa* (also called a *miliarium*), see Dunbabin 1993, 131.

other than the servants preparing for a normal, if luxurious, secular banquet.[19] From the House of Bacchus at Complutum in Hispania Tarraconensis comes a mosaic showing a row of six servants set against a plain ground (fig. 6). Identically dressed in long-sleeved, knee-length tunics, they stand in repetitive poses holding out wine cups, a napkin over their other arm. The mosaic decorates a corridor leading to a room recognizable from its layout as a triclinium. Guests would have passed over it on their way to the dining room, where they were greeted by a mosaic in which the drunken Dionysus stands amid his followers, while vintagers tread the grapes below: the theme of the offering of the wine, expressed realistically in the corridor, is repeated here in mythological guise.[20] Other house owners used the subject on mosaic thresholds, leading into rooms that must have served for dining and reception. At Uthina (Oudna) in Africa Proconsularis, a threshold panel, at the entrance to a large room in a peristyle house, showed two scantily clad servants, named as Myro and Victor, pouring wine from amphorae into a bowl held by a better-dressed central figure, named as Fructus, who is surely meant to be understood as the wine waiter (fig. 7).[21] Very similar is a mosaic from a house at Thugga (Dougga), also in Africa Proconsularis, where two large servants, one wearing only a loin cloth, the other a tunic *exomis* over one shoulder, pour wine from amphorae into the bowls held by two smaller attendants. Two young boys with long flowing hair wait at the sides, one to offer flowers, the other a towel and jug.[22]

[19] The suggestion that it was a cult banquet in honour of Isis was made by Herbig 1925. The only serious argument for the identification appears to be the resemblance of the knotted cloth worn by the central figure around his hips to the Isiac knot. However, as Baratte 1978, 73, points out, the Isiac knot is not worn in this position but is worn (by women) between the breasts. Slaves with girt-up tunics appear in Petronius, *Sat.* 60.8: *tres pueri candidas succincti tunicas*; Seneca, *De brev. vit.* 12.5: *quam diligenter exoletorum suorum tunicas succingant . . .*

[20] Fernández-Galiano 1984, I, 129–60 (the house); II, 135–86 (the mosaics). A date at the end of the fourth or beginning of the fifth century c.e. is proposed.

[21] Dunbabin 1978, 123. Fructus is normally taken to be the name of the owner of the house, but I now find this unlikely; the parallels suggest rather that he is to be taken as a higher-status servant, whose role is to offer the wine to the guests. Cf. also another more fragmentary mosaic from Uthina, also from a threshold, where two servants pour wine for two standing figures: Dunbabin 1978, 123, with references.

[22] Merlin 1919; Dunbabin 1978, 123, pl. 114; Blanchard-Lemée et al. 1995, 76–79, fig. 48. Probably mid to late third century c.e. Merlin 1919, 3, describes the house from which it came as rich with several rooms paved with mosaics; no further details of its location are given.

Another pair of servants of this type appear in the wall paintings of a house at Ephesos, one of the terraced houses by the Odeion, probably to be dated in the early fourth century C.E. (figs. 8–10).[23] In the doorway leading to a well-decorated room are painted two young men wearing knee-length tunics, one on each side, framed in separate panels. One holds up a glass beaker in one hand and has a towel over his left shoulder; the other holds up a big plate with a pile of figs, while in the other hand he holds two dead birds. Their role too is clearly to greet the entering guests and to symbolize the entertainment provided in the room through the food, drink, and towel that they offer. Unlike the other scenes so far discussed, however, the banqueting *dominus* also appears here; on the inner wall of the room, another panel contains a man reclining against a huge bolster, cup in one hand, the other stretched out towards a waiting servant who offers a silver plate laden with food. There is no attempt to unite this panel and the two servants at the doorway into a coherent scene; indeed, the difference in style between them suggests that they are the work of different artists. Nevertheless, a visual link would have carried the eye from the servants, standing at the entrance with their offerings, to the rear of the room where the *dominus* reclines at ease against the *stibadium* cushion and is served food and drink by yet another servant.[24]

All the paintings and mosaics discussed so far have come from a domestic setting: where identifiable, a dining room or a space immediately connected with one.[25] But the theme of the servants with their offerings of food and drink has a much wider use in late antiquity in a funerary setting. In many different parts of the Empire, and in both tomb

[23] Strocka 1995, 82–89.

[24] Solitary banqueters, as opposed to convivial groups, appear otherwise to be attested only in funerary contexts. Strocka 1995, 88–89, deduces from this that the dining figure here must have a commemorative function, perhaps as a portrayal of the owner's deceased father or ancestor represented as participating in the common meal. The scene seems to me to have an honorific function but not necessarily a commemorative one; the diner may well be represented as the (current) *dominus*. At this date the multivalent significance of scenes of dining leads to a great deal of mutual interchange among the motifs characteristic of the convivial and the solitary banquet; see Dunbabin 2003, chaps. 4 and 5.

[25] Only the room to which the Complutum corridor leads can be identified with certainty from its plan as a triclinium, but a similar use is probable for the Ephesos room and perhaps for that from which the Uthina mosaic came. The Schola Praeconum building may be classified as semi-public, but dining would have been an important part of its function as the seat of an association.

painting and funerary sculpture, processions of servants are found bearing food, drink, and other appropriate offerings.[26] Usually these are offered to the deceased, who may be represented reclining on the banqueting couch but may also stand to receive them, or may be placed in a separate panel; sometimes the servants appear alone. A number of Roman sarcophagi of the later third or early fourth century C.E. show rows of servants in attendance on their banqueting master or on the couple of master and mistress together. Best known is the very fine sarcophagus of Caecilius Vallianus in the Vatican, dated ca. 270 C.E. (fig. 11).[27] Vallianus reclines on his couch in the centre, with the table in front bearing a fish; a woman seated beside him plays a musical instrument, the *pandurium*. A maidservant with a vessel stands behind her, and on either side youthful male servants (six in all) hurry to serve their master. Three carry huge plates with various delicacies—a cake, a suckling pig, a fowl—a fourth carries the jug and basin used for handwashing; the two at either end bear live animals, a peacock and a hare. Baskets of roses stand at the ends beyond them. All the servants are similar in type, with long hair flowing over their shoulders, smooth cheeks, torques around their necks, soft shoes, and long-sleeved full tunics reaching to their knees.

Very similar scenes appear on other large sarcophagi, including some fine ones known only from drawings, while smaller and sometimes simplified versions appear on lids.[28] All include the processions of servants carrying plates of food and drinking vessels, though the number varies depending on their size and elaboration; the servant with the jug and basin for handwashing is also almost invariably present. A fine fragment in Berlin, for instance, contains a youthful servant, again with long flowing hair, full tunic fluttering around him, and torque, carrying a plate with a chicken; beside him are remains of two similar servants (fig. 12). One in Rome (Palazzo Mattei) has two such youths carrying fowl

[26] To the examples discussed below must be added the frequent use of the figure of the servant, male and female, on the funerary stelae and reliefs of the northwest and Danubian provinces: see Guerrier 1980 and cf. Piccottini 1977. These often draw on an iconography very similar to that used on the monuments discussed (e.g., Espérandieu 1913, no. 4313, from Metz, a long-haired youth bearing a dish with a fowl) and likewise can appear both in direct association with a banquet scene and isolated, for instance, on the lateral faces of a stele.

[27] Vatican, Museo Gregoriano Profano Inv. 9538/9539: Amedick 1991, 167–68, no. 286, pls. 15.2–4, 16–17. For a more detailed discussion of this sarcophagus, see Dunbabin 2003, chap. 4.

[28] Amedick 1991, 17–24.

and cake on elegant oval dishes and remains of a female servant holding up a drinking vessel (fig. 13).[29] Further details on these sarcophagi can include a scene of the preparation of the hot water, *calda*, to mix with the wine; bearers of garlands or baskets who offer flowers; and, once, a servant waving a flywhisk above his master's head (fig. 14). A lighter note is sometimes introduced by the children who play around the couch, recalling the fashion for keeping pert slave children or *delicia* as domestic pets.[30]

Tomb paintings, predominantly of the later third and fourth century, show the theme of the procession of servants used over a much wider geographical range. This theme seems to have been especially popular in Illyricum and the Danube provinces, but examples are found also in the eastern provinces.[31] As on the sarcophagi, it may be combined with a representation of a deceased individual, or the deceased couple, reclining alone on the couch, but also with a scene of the more convivial banquet, with a number of guests at the *stibadium*. Thus in a small vaulted tomb in the necropolis of Cheikh-Sou at Thessalonica, two guests reclined on a *sigma* couch, while three servants carrying plates approached along the surviving side wall.[32] In a tomb at Philippopolis (Plovdiv in Bulgaria), a couple (probably) reclined on a couch, while four servants stood in separate panels, holding plates with bread, fruit and fish, a wine jug and glass, and probably another vessel.[33] The somewhat larger hypogaeum known as the Tomb of the Orants at Constanza, the ancient Tomis, in Romania, contained scenes of the convivial banquet at the *stibadium* in the centre of both side walls, each with four or five guests; though damaged they were clearly directly comparable to the well-preserved Tomb of the Banquet in the same city, where the banqueting scene occupies the whole of the lunette on the end wall. In the latter, a single servant appears at either side of the banqueting scene, but the

[29] Berlin, Skulpturensammlung und Museum für byzantinische Kunst Inv. 2786: Amedick 1991, 124, no. 19, pl. 22.1–3. Rome, Palazzo Mattei: Amedick 1991, 156, no. 209, pl. 22.4. The female servant at the left is heavily restored.

[30] Flywhisk on a fragmentary lid of the beginning of the fourth century in the Museo Nazionale Romano: Amedick 1991, 150, no. 174, pl. 11.1. *Delicia*: Amedick 1991, 19–20; cf. Slater 1974, with earlier references; Nielsen 1990.

[31] For a survey, with further examples and references, see Valeva 2001, 180–85.

[32] Perdrizet 1905, 93–95, pl. II.

[33] Pillinger, Popova, and Zimmermann 1999, 42–46, no. 35, figs. 79–83. The paintings are now largely destroyed and known only from fragments and copies. The date appears to be Tetrarchic/early Constantinian.

Tomb of the Orants used the greater space available on the side walls to add separate panels with more prominent processions of servants: three survive on one side, perhaps in front of a sideboard, at least one and maybe traces of other servants on the other.[34]

In all the funerary scenes so far examined, the direct link between the servants and the banquet is maintained. By placing the servants in separate panels, they are given a more ceremonious emphasis than those who appear within the scene itself, and their number can be increased without danger of their swamping the guests. But the offerings that they bear or the implements they carry are directed unequivocally to their banqueting master or masters. Elsewhere, the link is looser. At Anemurium in Rough Cilicia (Tomb B. I 16), damaged paintings covered the walls and vault of a small chamber. Along one wall can be made out a row of three servants carrying plates or bowls in their covered hands, with remains of a fourth on the adjacent wall. The banquet itself was repre-sented on the vault above, where remains of a couch survive, together with fragmentary human figures and with the much larger bust of a woman. The scale of the other figures in the vault is much smaller than that of the row of servants below, and there is no direct connection between them; the viewer is left to associate them. The female bust, evidently the deceased, also reduces the resemblance to a unified ban-quet scene; the offerings of the servants must have been directed as much to her as to the figure on the couch.[35] A comparable division appears in a definitely Christian context in *cubiculum* 10 of the Cata-comb of Peter and Marcellinus in Rome. On the end wall, above a *loculus* opening, the small figure of a woman holding a drinking vessel reclines against a cushion. Two further small figures beneath stand in the orant position. Opposite, in upright panels on the entrance wall, are two much larger figures identifiable as servants, holding out a cup and a jug (fig. 15).[36]

[34] Tomb of the Orants: Barbet and Bucovală 1996, who suggest a date in the mid fourth century or later. The lunette wall contains paintings of two figures in the orant position; these are not sufficient in themselves to identify the tomb as Christian, but they do stress the honorific character of the paintings. For the Tomb of the Banquet, see Barbet 1994.

[35] Alföldi-Rosenbaum 1971, 112–17, 180, pls. 28–30, who suggests a date for these paintings of the end of the third or first decades of the fourth century. She identifies the best preserved of the servants as a woman; but it is more likely to be a long-haired effeminate boy, like many other figures discussed here (below nn. 45–48).

[36] Wilpert 1903, 477, pl. 107, 1.3; Deckers, Seeliger, and Mietke 1987, 209–10, no. 10. An inscription divided between the three figures on the end wall reads [B]INKENTIA, pre-sumably the woman's name.

More abstract still was the treatment of the theme in a painted rock-cut tomb from Sidon, now destroyed but known from nineteenth-century drawings. Instead of the deceased owner reclining on a couch, he appeared standing alone on the end wall, while six servants stood along the side walls on the pillars left between the openings for *loculi*.[37] The general effect of the paintings resembles the room in the House on the Caelian, except that the servants were not hurrying forward but standing frontally. They were dressed in the usual full long-sleeved tunics, and several had long curly hair. They held great silver dishes of food: a large fowl or a couple of smaller birds, a fish, or a cake. Beside them were written their names, some chosen for their significance: Oinophilos (evidently the wine bearer, though the object he holds is lost), Glykon (with the cake), Kalokeros (bearing two small birds), Helicon (with half a fish), Petenos (with fowl), and Nereus (with a fish). Two female figures flanked the figure of the master; one held a scroll and probably symbolized his learning and culture, the other stood beside a tall amphora and may represent the joy of the banquet. This is, therefore, in no sense a scene of a banquet in progress, yet the servants are hardly offering their gifts to the visitor in the same way as those on the domestic paintings and mosaics set at the entrance to a dining room. The deceased owner of the tomb, who held what is probably meant as a scroll, must evidently be understood as the recipient of their offerings; the effect is honorific, designed to glorify the wealth, happiness, and culture of the dead patron, to whom all these good things are brought. There is doubtless an allusion to the funerary banquet celebrated by the survivors in commemoration of the dead and also to the offerings of food and drink that might be made at the tomb. At the same time, the servants with their elegant appearance and the rich food borne on elaborate silver dishes serve as a mark of the status achieved by the deceased in life and glorified in death.[38]

Sometimes the iconography is reduced to a bare minimum of its essential elements: the deceased and a servant. A small brick-built tomb of the first half of the fourth century at Viminacium (Stari Kostolac, in Serbia) contains just two painted figures: at one end a male servant advancing with a huge dish of circular loaves, at the other, the upper part of a richly dressed woman, evidently the one buried in the tomb (fig. 16). The two figures together are sufficient to convey the main message; the

---

[37] Barbet, Gatier, and Lewis 1997; the date may be third or fourth century.

[38] For further discussion of the multivalent significance of such scenes of the banquet in funerary contexts, see Dunbabin 2003, chap. 4.

side walls between them contain peacocks drinking from a vase, a common funerary motif which can evoke both luxury and elegance in this life and the refreshment of paradise in the next.[39] The painting in a Christian tomb at Thessalonica shows the deceased couple, identified by inscription as Flavios and Eustorgia, standing on the end wall, both richly dressed, the man in tunic and chlamys, the woman with necklace and jewelled headdress. Two small figures, both boys in short tunics, stand between them, their hands grasping a jug on a stand, while one holds a conical beaker. They have usually been taken to be the children of the deceased couple, but the gesture with the wine jug shows that they must be attendants serving their masters wine. An old woman at the side is labelled "Aurelia Procla mother of all"; she is perhaps also a servant.[40]

II

The physical beauty and elegant appearance required of the attendants at the banquets of the rich and fashionable form a familiar theme already in the literature of the early Empire. Philo of Alexandria devotes several paragraphs of his attack on the luxury of Italian-style banquets to the "waiting slaves of the greatest comeliness and beauty, so that they seem to have come less for the sake of service than to please the sight of the beholders." He distinguishes three groups: the young boys who pour the wine; the slightly older boys who carry the water, bathed and anointed, their faces painted with cosmetics, their long thick hair plaited and woven, or trimmed in a special cut, their brilliant white tunics cobweb-fine and reaching below the knee; and the youths whose beards are just beginning to grow, magnificently dressed up for the heavier work, as proof of the hosts' opulence.[41] Latin authors of the first and early second centuries C.E. give similar accounts of the table servants of the rich. Seneca, for instance, speaks of the wine server, adorned like a woman, or

[39] Korać 1991; Valeva 2001, 182–83, figs. 36–37. For peacocks, see, e.g., Schneider 1983, 49–50.

[40] Pelekanidis 1969, 230–35, figs. 25–30; for the inscriptions see Feissel 1983, 121–22, nos. 124, 125. The inscription of Aurelia Procla is dedicatory, so even if the term "mother of all" is meant to be honorific rather than literal, she does not play the same role as the servants in the other paintings. The early fourth-century date proposed by Pelekanidis is accepted by Feissel.

[41] Philo *de vit. cont.* 50–52: on this passage, see Fless 1995, 58–59; Pollini 1999, 35–36; Pollini 2002, 54–55.

of the long-haired boy who holds out a translucent cup to his master.[42] Juvenal similarly has his "flower of Asia," a boy bought for more than the entire fortune of the kings of Rome, who cannot be expected to pour wine for a poor man; while Martial's newly rich Aper, previously censorious towards drunks, now revels in his open-work cups and five long-haired boys.[43] Especially stressed is the long, beautiful hair of these boys, so that terms such as *capillati, comati*, or *criniti* are sufficient to identify the whole category of luxurious table servants; other sources refer to their fine complexions and smooth cheeks, and more generally to their delicacy and beauty.[44]

The appearance of an iconographic type corresponding to the luxurious slaves described in these accounts has recently been studied by Friederike Fless. She identifies a type of youthful figure in short, full tunic with long wavy hair falling to the shoulders. Used for the attendants (*ministri*) at public sacrifices, this type also appears occasionally from the late Flavian period for the servants in banquet scenes.[45] On the late Flavian funerary altar of Q. Socconius Felix in Rome, for instance, three such boys appear in attendance on their reclining master and mistress, bearing wine jug, towel, and garland.[46] Fless further identifies such slaves on a remarkable mosaic in Capua (fig. 17). It shows a group of youthful figures (fifteen survive) wearing short blue tunics and with long hair in a variety of hairstyles, several very feminine in appearance; they stand in rows with an older man behind them. Several of the hairstyles became fashionable in the late Flavian period, allowing the mosaic to be dated in the late first or early second century C.E. The scene has often been interpreted as a choir, perhaps of girls, or a school class. Fless suggests, rather, that it is to be seen as a representation of the slaves from a *paedagogium* where luxury household slaves were trained in the skills

---

[42] Sen. *Ep.* 47.7: *alius vini minister in muliebrem modum ornatus*; *Ep.* 119.14: *quam crinitus puer et quam perlucidum tibi poculum porrigat . . .*

[43] Juv. 5.56–62; Mart. 12.70.9: *o quantum diatreta valent et quinque comati!*

[44] Cf. also Luc. *Sat.* 24 on the pretty long-haired boys to serve the wine, whom the rich call Hyakinthos or Achilles or Narkissos; Tac. *Ann.* 15.69, on the *decora servitia et pari aetate* owned by the consul Vestinus, who provoked Nero's fatal enmity; and Sen. *Ep* 95.24, cited in n. 6 above. For further sources, and the use of terms such as *glabri, exoleti*, or *delicati*, see Fless 1995, 58–63; Pollini 1999, 29–36; Pollini 2002, 53–57 (especially on the hairstyles of such slaves); also Marquardt 1886, 146–47; Garrido-Hory 1981, 93–95, 147–52.

[45] Fless 1995, 38–45, 56–63; also Balty 1982; Pollini 2002, 53–62.

[46] Fless 1995, 56, pl. 25.1; Goethert 1969.

and arts of service.[47] Regrettably, nothing is known of the original location of the mosaic, which might help to cast light on its function. It differs from the later representations of the rows of waiting servants in the absence of any indication of offerings held by the standing figures; there is no reference to a banquet, nor to any other specific context at which their services are rendered. It shows, therefore, that the iconographic motif of the luxury household servants was indeed known at this date, but it remains a puzzling unicum.[48]

The theme of the rows of servants with offerings is, however, anticipated at least once in domestic decoration of the mid first century, though on a smaller scale: among the paintings of the Casa dei Vettii at Pompeii (VI 15.1). In the atrium (c) here, a row of window-like openings in the socle contains small figures of children holding out various objects (fig. 18).[49] These include a tray of food, with a jug and situla alongside; a jug and basin; a garland; a metal kantharos; a semicircular cista; and an incense burner. Some of the objects, therefore, resemble those of secular festivity, such as are held by later figures of servants, but others seem to belong in the context of ritual. The children, who appear to be very young, occupy only an insignificant position low down on the walls. They can in no way be compared with the impressive rows of serving figures who constitute by themselves the main element of the decoration in paintings such as those of the Schola Praeconum or the House on the Caelian.

The type of the beautiful, long-haired boy is adopted widely in these later paintings and is used especially for the wine server, who is

[47] Fless 1995, 60, pl. 25.2; for earlier publication and interpretations of the mosaic, see the works cited in her n. 425. Several of the boys have hairstyles characteristic of Flavian female portraiture, providing a *terminus post quem* for the mosaic. Fless' convincing interpretation is accepted also by Pollini 2002, 60.

[48] Fless 1995, 63–69, and Pollini 2002, 53–62, both discuss a group of portrait busts of long-haired youths, apparently dating from the mid to late first century c.e., for which an identification as portraits of *delicati* or servile ministrants is suggested. In the absence of any context for these portraits, they are less useful for the present discussion; but, if the identification is correct, they too show the existence of the iconographic type of long-haired slave boy long before it became commonly used for the waiting servants carrying banquet apparatus.

[49] Baldassarre, Lanzilotta, and Salomi 1994, 475–80, who think they show the preparation for a religious ceremony; Fless 1995, 57, pls. 26–29. Two other figures in the series show a boy with a cup offering a drink to a guinea fowl and a wreathed child wrapped in a cloak; Fless argues that these genre motifs make an allusion to cult less likely.

shown in the Caelian paintings, for instance, as much more expensively dressed than the others. But it is also used more widely for boys serving other functions. The other servants in the Caelian paintings, who hurry forward carrying their huge dishes, include two with long flowing hair, while the rest have shorter but still curly locks. In the tomb at Sidon at least three have shoulder-length locks, and one wears his hair in a chignon on top of his head.[50] On the sarcophagus of Caecilius Vallianus and many of the other sarcophagi with banquet scenes, all the male servants alike belong to the long-haired type.[51] Elsewhere there is a distinction of type and function: on the Thugga mosaic, for instance, the two boys who bear flowers and the jug and towel for handwashing are long-haired; the figures with bowls in the centre are shorter haired (one has a pony tail) but still finely dressed; while the two huge figures with amphorae, in *exomis* and loin cloth, are clearly meant to indicate a different type of servant, noted for strength rather than elegance.[52] Some of the scenes, therefore, take pains to distinguish various categories, reflecting a hierarchy of status within the ranks of the servants themselves. But in others, especially the later ones, the attractions of a uniform presentation of the serried rows of attendants outweigh the desire to differentiate; in particular, the most privileged and valued type, the elegant long-haired boy, is repeated and multiplied.[53]

Literary sources stress the diversity of tasks performed by the servants as much as the visual effect of the crowds of beautiful attendants.[54] The degree of attention paid to this aspect in late antique art varies. Alongside the wine server and the attendants with dishes of food, several new types appear, especially on the sarcophagi. One of the most important is the servant carrying jug and basin for handwashing, who becomes one of the most frequent figures in banquet scenes, almost as

[50] Caelian: above nn. 12–14; Sidon: n. 37. The type is also used for the wine server in a number of scenes of the banquet in progress, such as the mosaic from Shahba-Philippopolis discussed by Balty 1982.

[51] Sarcophagi: nn. 27–29.

[52] Thugga: n. 22; for the figure in *exomis*, cf. the mosaics from Carthage (above n. 19) and Uthina (above n. 21).

[53] See further below nn. 61–65, 71, on the appearance of the same type of elegant pageboy in other contexts, and Balty 1982 for the use of the type to characterize an especially privileged category of servants.

[54] Cf. D'Arms 1991, 172–73, with nn. 3–13; also Marquardt 1886, 146–47. Add Clem. Alex. *Paed.* 3.4.26.1–2.

indispensable as the boy with the wine.[55] Others may include the servants
distributing garlands or flowers, as on the Thugga mosaic; the figure with
a flywhisk, on one of the sarcophagi; and figures who operate the apparatus for heating the water.[56] The more formal representations, however,
again prefer a more uniform presentation, concentrating on the offering
of the wine and the great dishes laden with a variety of food. The
magnificence of the silver dishes also corresponds to the fashions of late
antique society; their prominence reflects the part played by huge luxury
plates in the treasures of silverware from the fourth century.[57] So, when
Sidonius Apollinaris in the mid fifth century composes a set of verses
about a banquet, he singles out for mention the servants bearing the
engraved silver dishes on their laden shoulders.[58]

III

The processions of luxury slaves are not confined to scenes of the banquet in the art of this period; they appear also in other contexts, foremost
among them the bath. Here an iconography developed which focused
particularly upon the female bather, who is shown surrounded by rows of
attendant handmaids bearing mirrors, perfume flasks, basins, and other
toilet articles.[59] The theme is illustrated very clearly on the silver Casket
of Projecta from the Esquiline Treasure, produced in Rome in the middle

[55] For the jug-and-basin set as the equipment for handwashing, see Nuber 1972, esp.
83–90, 117–21, 128–29. Like the long-haired attendants themselves, the equipment belongs
originally in the sacral sphere (Fless 1995, 15–17), but it is represented repeatedly, and
often shown in use, in late antique scenes of the banquet: cf. Dunbabin 2003, chap. 5.

[56] Thugga: above n. 22. Figure with flywhisk: above n. 30. Water heating: cf. Dunbabin
1993, 129–40. Another new type found on some of the sarcophagi is the servant with the
corkscrew locks that characterize Roman representations of black Africans and recall
literary sources that refer to fashions for exotic Aethiopian slaves: cf. Amedick 1991, 21.

[57] Cf. Baratte 1990; S. Martin-Kilcher in Cahn and Kaufmann-Heinimann 1984,
393– 404.

[58] Sid. Ap. *Ep.* 9.13.54–57: "geruli caput plicantes / anaglyptico metallo / epulas
superbiores / umeris ferant onustis."

[59] A comparatively early example of this iconography was found in the paintings of
the baths from beneath the Piazza dei Cinquecento in Rome near Stazione Termini.
Against an architectural setting reminiscent of the paintings of the Schola Praeconum
appeared figures of nude women bathing, attended by clothed and nude servants, male and
female, with bathing equipment; they belong apparently to a late Antonine/Severan phase
of decoration. See Barbera and Paris 1996, 122–27, 158–64; Mielsch 2001, 108–10.

or second half of the fourth century.[60] Around the body of the casket, a
series of elegant maidservants carries offerings to the lady enthroned in
the centre of the front, who may be taken as meant for Projecta herself;
among them, two pageboys carry candles, the same type of long-haired
boy in flowing calf-length tunics found in the context of the banquet
scenes (figs. 19, 20). Another silver casket for carrying toilet flasks formed
part of the Sevso Treasure. It has a cylindrical body, with the lady enthroned on the front, at the centre of a procession of attendants carrying
bath articles: among them is a casket identical to the real object it
decorates, as well as basins, vessels, mirror, and what seems to be a large
clothes basket. On the back is a scene of the bath itself, with a woman
undressing helped by a maidservant and two nude women.[61] Scenes like
these are clearly designed to convey a compliment to the beauty and
elegance of the lady represented. Her toilette is shown as a ceremonial
occasion, the opportunity for the display of fine clothes, magnificent
jewellery, and rich silver vessels, while the bathing scenes imply comparisons with Venus and the Nymphs, models of feminine beauty and grace.[62]
      But the setting for this display is not confined to the private sphere.
On the back panel of the lid of the Projecta casket, the lady appears
walking amid further attendants, another of the long-haired boys among
them; they accompany her to a columned building with a mass of domes
(fig. 21). The scene is usually, and I believe rightly, now interpreted as the
procession of the lady to the baths, escorted by her personal servants
carrying the bathing apparatus.[63] A bath procession of this type is certainly

      [60] Barbier 1961; Shelton 1981, 27–28, 72–75, pls. 1–11; Schneider 1983, 3–38. For the
date of the treasure, see the discussions of Cameron 1985 and Shelton 1985.
      [61] Mundell Mango and Bennett 1994, 445–73, no. 14, with a date proposed in the fifth
century. Three of the maids on the Casket of Projecta likewise carry caskets comparable to
the Casket itself, but they do not mirror its form as closely as the one here does.
      [62] Cf. also the more abbreviated scene of the lady with two maidservants and a
variety of bathing apparatus on the mosaic from Sidi Ghrib, near Carthage: Ennabli 1986,
42–44; Blanchard-Lemée et al. 1995, 155, fig. 116. The bathing women on the Sevso casket
may also be compared to the women on a silver bucket in the Museo Archeologico
Nazionale in Naples, Inv. 25289, supposed to come from Herculaneum but clearly no earlier
than the late third or fourth century: Pozzi 1986, 214–15, no. 63, pls. pp. 98–100 (dated there
to the end of the second to the beginning of the third century, much too early); Pirzio Biroli
Stefanelli 1991, 277, no. 108, figs. 164–66. The parallel with Venus is explicit on the Projecta
casket, where the front panel of the lid shows the toilet of Venus, borne in her shell by
Tritons, immediately above, and directly comparable to, the figure of Projecta beneath.
      [63] For the interpretation as a bath procession, see Barbier 1961, followed by Shelton
1981. Schneider 1983 unconvincingly retains the older interpretation of the scenes as all
concerned with the ritual of a wedding.

represented on one of the mosaics of the villa at Piazza Armerina, which paved the vestibule leading from the peristyle to the bathing rooms (fig. 22). Here a magnificently dressed lady, rich in jewellery and with fashionable fourth-century hairstyle, is accompanied by two boys, also richly dressed in ornamented tunics and cloaks and with long, flowing blond hair—not the lady's sons, as often taken, but two more of the elegant pageboys. Two maidservants complete the group, one carrying a chest evidently full of clean clothes, the other a casket on a chain and a satchel.[64] Other mosaics in the bathing rooms of the villa show the bathers surrounded by servants who assist them to dress and bring towels, clothes, and apparatus for the bath. Around the frigidarium opens a series of apsidal alcoves, which probably served as changing rooms, their pavements decorated with appropriate scenes. On one, a bather sits wrapped in a towel, while two servants bring clothes. On another, a splendidly dressed man is preparing to put on a fine silk scarf, while a boy kneels at his feet to adjust his sandals, and a second—another of the elegant page boys—holds out a further fine garment.[65]

A visit to the baths provided one of the main settings for ostentatious display by the rich. The theme recurs frequently in the sources and perhaps especially during the later empire. Ammianus Marcellinus, in the chapters that he devotes to an attack on the vices of the Roman aristocrats, paints a vivid picture of the great nobles arriving at the baths, resplendent in silken garments and followed by a crowd of slaves drawn up in troops, or entering the bathing rooms with an escort of fifty servants.[66] Christian writers such as Clement of Alexandria denounce especially the luxurious ostentation of rich women at the baths, the innumer-

---

[64] Carandini, Ricci, and de Vos 1982, 331–34, Room 21, fig. 200, pl. 55; for the identification of the two boys as prestige servants rather than her sons, see Barbier 1961, 22–23; Balty 1982, 304–5.

[65] Carandini, Ricci, and de Vos 1982, 343–56, Room 4a–i, esp. 4b2, pl. 59, 4f, pl. 58. The mosaics have been extensively restored in several phases in antiquity, and many of the other alcoves are very fragmentary. For colour illustrations of these scenes, see Gentili 1959, pls. 5, 6. Cf. also the bathing attendants named as Titus and Cassius (in the vocative) on the mosaic of a room perhaps serving as a *cella unguentaria*, along with another attendant rubbing down a naked bather: Carandini, Ricci, and de Vos 1982, 359–62, Room 5, pl. 61.

[66] Amm. Marc. 28.4.8–9; cf. also 28.4.19. Earlier Plutarch includes among the signs of moderation of the *sophron* that he does not make himself offensive by the number of servants who attend him in the baths (*Mor.* 823B), while Lucian's Nigrinus similarly criticizes those who bring large numbers of attendants to the baths or who employ servants to walk before them to warn them of obstacles in their path (*Nigr.* 34). See more generally Fagan 1999, 215–17.

able objects of gold and silver that they carry around with them, and the silverware with which they parade in the baths.[67] The monuments make it clear that these attacks are not mere conventional tropes. Silver vessels such as the caskets in the Esquiline and Sevso treasures were not intended only for domestic use but to be displayed before an admiring public as their owners proceeded in state around the bathing establishments; the servants who are represented on them were likewise an essential part of the display. The elegant turnout of the servants is as conspicuous in these scenes as in those of the banquet. The mosaics in particular, with their greater use of colour, illustrate the splendour with which the servants, male and female, are dressed—the rich fabrics, embroidered ornament, the jewellery of the maidservants, and their fashionable hairstyles. The throngs of servants were there, not just to serve, but also to be seen; the visual impact of the bathing ceremonies of the rich is brought emphatically before the observers' eyes.[68]

The most telling example of the servant theme in late antique art takes as its context neither the banquet nor the baths. It comes from a chamber tomb at Durostorum on the Danube (the modern Silistra in Bulgaria), probably dating from around the middle of the fourth century C.E. (fig. 23).[69] The walls of the tomb are painted with a series of panels containing half-lifesize figures: two processions of servants, male and female, directed towards the two figures in the central panel of the end wall. These are clearly the owners of the tomb; the man wears official costume with chlamys, fibula, tunic, and trousers, the woman a dalmatic and a turban-like headdress. The female servants carry objects destined for the female toilet similar to those seen on the silver caskets and mosaics just discussed: a jug and basin, a perfume container on a chain, a towel, and a mirror (fig. 24). However, the male servants introduce quite different associations. They carry garments resembling those worn by the master on the end wall and that belong to the official costume of the late

[67] Clem. Alex. *Paed.* 3.5.31.1–2.

[68] From another standpoint, the servants could be regarded as invisible, at least to their owners. Ammianus' aristocrat, on entering the baths with his fifty servants, is represented as calling out petulantly *ubi ubi sunt nostri?* (Amm. Marc. 28.4. 9), while Clement thunders disapprovingly against the practice of rich women bathing naked in the presence of their male slaves—in effect ignoring either their presence or their maleness (Clem. Alex. *Paed.* 3.5.32.3).

[69] Dimitrov 1961; Schneider 1983, 39–55; Valeva 1990; Pillinger, Popova, and Zimmermann 1999, 22–28, with full previous bibliography. The more precise dating of the tomb within the fourth century is problematic, with arguments advanced for the earlier and later part of that century; the question remains unresolved.

Roman state: a pair of voluminous breeches and a pair of shoes, a chlamys complete with fibula projecting from its edge, and a heavy metal belt (fig. 25). The fourth servant turns towards the one holding the belt and stretches out his arms, covered with a cloth as a sign of respect, to receive it.[70] Three of the male servants are dressed comparatively simply in sleeved short tunics and leggings, with torques or neck rings with pendants around their necks. The last, holding up the chlamys, is once again an elegant pageboy with long blond hair and ornamented tunic.[71] While the female servants, therefore, serve to pay the customary compliments to the beauty of the lady, the male servants are shown as investing the master with his official uniform of office; they shift the point of reference to the public art of the late Roman state.

IV

When Ammianus Marcellinus composed his denunciation of the luxury and decadence of the Roman aristocracy of the late fourth century, the terms of his attack had been common currency among moralists and satirists for many centuries. The picture that he paints of the appearance of the great nobles in public, "dragging behind their backs troops of household slaves like bands of brigands," was hardly new.[72] For the elite of the earlier empire, the possession of crowds of luxury household servants had played an essential role in the process of self-representation and social emulation. Nevertheless, in the art of that period, the emphasis lay elsewhere: on public office and its manifestations. It was characteristic of late antiquity that, alongside the emergence of a new artistic lan-

---

[70] On the significance of the gesture with covered hands, see, e.g., Alföldi 1970, 33–35; Schneider 1983, 43–44. Pillinger, Popova, and Zimmermann 1999, 25, argued that the *orbiculi* with which the cloth is decorated mean that it must be an article of clothing (they suggest a tunic), but they may simply be a further honorific sign.

[71] Torques are worn also by the servants on some of the sarcophagi, notably that of Caecilius Vallianus in the Vatican (n. 27) and the fragment in Berlin (n. 29); similar but simpler neckbands are seen on the servants at Complutum (n. 20). They should not be taken to allude directly to any specific ethnic origin for the servants, any more than the long blond hair of the pageboy with the cloak (sometimes taken to suggest a Germanic origin, for instance, by Dimitrov 1961, 50; but cf. Balty 1982; Fless 1995, 61). See also Wrede 1972, 85–87, with further parallels for torques and neckbands worn by slaves (and others in late antiquity), though he too sees the practice as an allusion to a barbarian origin. But while they may have originally have been intended to identify the wearers as exotic northerners, they evidently came to be used more widely as an ornament for luxury servants generally.

[72] Amm. Marc. 14.6.16: *familiarium agmina tamquam praedatorios globos post terga trahentes.*

guage for the portrayal of new distinctions of rank and status, there appeared also a much greater emphasis on the visual presentation of the more "private" realm. The rituals of the daily life of members of the elite—their highly ceremonial rules of comportment—found appropriate expression in the more abstract and formulaic styles increasingly favoured in contemporary art.[73]

The theme of the rows of waiting servants seems to have enjoyed its main period of popularity between the late third and the late fourth century. The individual components of these scenes often drew on motifs that had been in use for many centuries, as the example of the figure of the long-haired servant illustrates. But their more restrained use at earlier periods fell far short of the honorific effect now produced through the isolated presentation or emphatic repetition of these motifs. There can be little doubt that the inspiration for such a mode of representation came from the art of the imperial court. Among the subjects that appear with increasing frequency on state monuments and in official imperial art from the time of the Tetrarchs onwards is that of the procession of bearers of gifts. Not only conquered or suppliant barbarians kneel with their offerings at the emperor's feet, but rows of personified provinces may appear bearing bowls of tribute.[74] The theme was also adopted into Christian iconography for scenes of the Adoration of the Magi, who hurry forward carrying their gifts in a way very similar to some of the servants discussed in this paper, and later even for processions of apostles and martyrs bearing their wreaths as offerings to Christ.[75] Individual elements, such as the bearers' covered hands, are also derived from the imperial iconography.[76] Here, as in many other respects, the upper classes of the late empire formed their images of status in emulation of the imperial model—the art of the "private" sphere reflects the ceremonies and formulae of the imperial realm.[77]

---

[73] On this phenomenon, see esp. Warland 1994; more generally, Schneider 1983. I use "private" here (in the absence of any other convenient English word) to signify "non-official"; it is obvious that no aspects of the life of a member of the Roman elite were strictly private in the sense in which we would normally understand the word today.

[74] Cf. Ploumis 1997. Note especially the figures of personified dioceses carrying bowls heaped with coins, their hands partially or fully veiled, who appear among the insignia of the praetorian prefects in the insignia of the *Notitia Dignitatum*: Berger 1981, 37–39, figs. 2, 47.

[75] Ploumis 1997, 136–38; Cumont 1932–33.

[76] Above n. 70.

[77] Comparable also are the scenes of the offering of rural produce or the gifts of the seasons by rural servants or *coloni* to their masters which become popular at the same period; see, for example, the late fourth-century mosaic of Dominus Iulius from Carthage: Veyne 1981; Schneider 1983, 68–84; Raeck 1987.

Similar emulation operated in turn within the different levels of the elite. Some of the works discussed above were designed to meet the requirements of the higher members of the aristocracy. Thus the villa of Piazza Armerina is now generally accepted to have been the seat of a great family of Roman aristocrats; the casket of the Esquiline Treasure was produced for a member of the eminent Roman family of the Turcii and his bride.[78] But the great majority belong lower down on the socio-economic scale: to the owners of spacious but not exceptionally wealthy houses in small towns of the African or Spanish provinces or to the proprietors of tombs, which again are prosperous but not unduly lavish. In the case of the Silistra tomb, the man's costume suggests an identity as a holder of office in the imperial service but not at its highest levels. It is obviously impossible to estimate the numbers of household servants that such men and women would have actually owned. Certainly they could not compete with the troops belonging to one of Ammianus' Roman aristocrats or to another member of a great Roman family, the younger Melania, who is said to have freed eight thousand slaves upon adopting an ascetic life.[79] But the iconographic formulae of luxurious living, and of service readily available and offered, could be used as effectively to suit the aspirations of those lower down on the scale as they could to convey the lifestyle of the truly great.[80]

McMASTER UNIVERSITY
e-mail: dunbabin@mcmaster.ca

[78] Piazza Armerina: Carandini, Ricci, and de Vos 1982, 27–52 (though the specific identification of the owner as L. Aradius Valerius Proculus Populonius proposed there has not found universal acceptance); for the whole controversy over the ownership of the villa, see the works cited in Dunbabin 1999, 132–33, nn. 8–9. For the Esquiline Treasure and the casket of Projecta, see the papers of Cameron 1985 and Shelton 1985: their disagreements over detail do not affect the context for which the casket was produced.

[79] Melania: Palladius, *Histoire Lausiaque* 61.5 (Lucot); many other slaves chose to remain in the service of her brother, and a number of female servants evidently remained as her companions in asceticism. The number eight thousand (which naturally should not be taken too literally) presumably included large numbers of rural slaves; nevertheless, her personal staff was evidently vast.

[80] This article is dedicated to the memory of John D'Arms in recollection of many enjoyable and provocative discussions of Roman banqueting customs. I am grateful to many other colleagues and friends with whom I have discussed the subject of the paper, and to all those who provided photographs, especially to V. M. Strocka. I also acknowledge with gratitude the continuing support of the Social Sciences and Humanities Research Council of Canada.

BIBLIOGRAPHY

Abbreviations of journal titles follow those of *L'Année Philologique*.

Alföldi, Andreas. 1970. *Die monarchische Repräsentation im römischen Kaiserreiche*. Darmstadt: Wissenschaftliche Buchgesellschaft.

Alföldi-Rosenbaum, Elisabeth. 1971. *Anamur Nekropolü: The Necropolis of Anamurium*. Ankara: Türk Tarih Kurumu Yayınlarından. Seri 6, no. 12.

Amedick, Rita. 1991. *Die Sarkophage mit Darstellungen aus dem Menschenleben* 4. *Vita Privata*. Die antiken Sarkophagreliefs 1.4. Berlin: Gebr. Mann.

Baldassarre, Ida, T. Lanzilotta, and S. Salomi, eds. 1994. *Pompei. Pitture e mosaici* V. *Regio VI, Parte II*. Rome: Istituto della Enciclopedia Italiana.

Balty, Janine. 1982. "*Paedagogiani*-pages, de Rome à Byzance." In *Rayonnement grec. Hommages à Charles Delvoye*, ed. L. Hadermann-Misguich, G. Raepsaet, 299–312, pls. 28–30. Brussels: Éditions de l'Université de Bruxelles.

Baratte, François. 1978. *Catalogue des mosaïques romaines et paléochrétiennes du musée du Louvre*. Paris: Édition de la Réunion des musées nationaux.

———. 1990. "La vaisselle de bronze et d'argent sur les monuments figurés romains. Documents anciens et nouveaux." *BSAF* 1990:89–108.

Barbera, Mariarosaria, and Rita Paris, eds. 1996. *Antiche stanze: Un quartiere di Roma Imperiale nella zona di Termini*. Milan: Mondadori.

Barbet, Alix. 1994. "Le tombeau du banquet de Constanța en Roumanie." In *Édifices et peintures, IVe au XIe siècles*. Colloque CNRS 1992, Auxerre: 25–47.

Barbet, Alix, and Mihai Bucovală. 1996. "L'hypogée paléochrétien des Orants à Constanța (Roumanie), l'ancienne Tomis." *MEFRA* 108:105–58.

Barbet, Alix, Pierre-Louis Gatier, and Norman Lewis. 1997. "Un tombeau peint inscrit de Sidon." *Syria* 74:141–60.

Barbier, Edmond. 1961. "La signification du cortège représenté sur le couvercle du coffret de 'Projecta'." *CArch* 12:7–33.

Berger, Pamela. 1981. *The Insignia of the Notitia Dignitatum*. Outstanding Dissertations in the Fine Arts. New York: Garland.

Blanchard-Lemée, Michèle, M. Ennaïfer, H. Slim, and L. Slim. 1995. *Sols de l'Afrique romaine: Mosaïques de Tunisie*. Paris: Imprimerie nationale.

Bollmann, Beate. 1998. *Römische Vereinshäuser: Untersuchungen zu den Scholae der römischen Berufs-, Kult- und Augustalen-Kollegien in Italien*. Mainz: von Zabern.

Cagiano de Azevedo, Michelangelo. 1947–49. "Osservazioni sulle pitture di un edificio romano di Via dei Cerchi." *RPAA* 23/4:253–58.

Cahn, Herbert, and Annemarie Kaufmann-Heinimann, eds. 1984. *Der spätrömische Silberschatz von Kaiseraugst*. Derendingen: Habegger.

Cameron, Alan. 1985. "The Date and Ownership of the Esquiline Treasure." *AJA* 89:135–45.

Carandini, Andrea, Andreina Ricci, and Mariette de Vos. 1982. *Filosofiana: The Villa of Piazza Armerina*. Palermo: S. F. Flaccovio.

Cumont, Franz. 1932–33. "L'adoration des Mages et l'art triomphal de Rome." *MPAA* 3:81–105, pls. 1–9.

D'Arms, John H. 1991. "Slaves at Roman Convivia." In *Dining in a Classical Context*, ed. W. J. Slater, 171–83. Ann Arbor: University of Michigan Press.

Deckers, Johannes, H. R. Seeliger, and Gabriele Mietke. 1987. *Die Katakombe "Santi Marcellino e Pietro." Repertorium der Malereien*. Roma sotterranea Cristiana 6. Vatican City: Aschendorffsche Verlagsbuchhandlung.

Dentzer, Jean-Marie. 1982. *Le motif du banquet couché dans le proche-orient et le monde grec du VIIe au IVe siècle avant J.-C.* Bibliothèque des Écoles françaises d'Athènes et de Rome 246. Rome.

Dimitrov, Dimiter. 1961. "Le système décoratif et la date des peintures murales du tombeau antique de Silistra." *CArch* 12:35–52.

Donati, Angela, ed. 1998. *Romana pictura: La pittura romana dalle origini all'età bizantina*. Rimini: Electa.

Dunbabin, Katherine. 1978. *The Mosaics of Roman North Africa*. Oxford: Clarendon Press.

———. 1993. "Wine and Water at the Roman Convivium." *JRA* 6:116–41.

———. 1999. *Mosaics of the Greek and Roman World*. Cambridge: Cambridge University Press.

———. 2003. *The Roman Banquet: Images of Conviviality*. Cambridge: Cambridge University Press (forthcoming).

Ennabli, Abdelmagid. 1986. "Les thermes du thiase marin de Sidi Ghrib (Tunisie)." *MMAI* 68:1– 59.

Espérandieu, Émile. 1913. *Recueil général des bas-reliefs, statues et bustes de la Gaule romaine* 5. *Belgique—première partie*. Paris.

Fabricius, Johanna. 1999. *Die hellenistischen Totenmahlreliefs. Grabrepräsentation und Wertvorstellungen in ostgriechischen Städten*. Studien zur antiken Stadt 3. Munich: Pfeil.

Fagan, Garrett. 1999. *Bathing in Public in the Roman World*. Ann Arbor: University of Michigan Press.

Feissel, Denis. 1983. *Recueil des inscriptions chrétiennes de Macédoine du IIIe au VIe siècle. BCH* suppl. 8. Athens-Paris: de Boccard.

Fernández-Galiano, Dimas. 1984. *Complutum* I. *Excavaciónes*. II. *Mosaicos*. Excavaciónes arqueológicas en España. Madrid: Ministerio de Cultura.

Fless, Friederike. 1995. *Opferdiener und Kultmusiker auf stadtrömischen historischen Reliefs*. Mainz: von Zabern.

Fröhlich, Thomas. 1991. *Lararien- und Fassadenbilder in den Vesuvstädten*. Mainz: von Zabern.

Garrido-Hory, M. 1981. *Martial et l'esclavage*. Annales littéraires de l'Université de Besançon 255. Paris: Les Belles Lettres.

Gentili, G. V. 1959. *La villa erculia di Piazza Armerina: I mosaici figurati*. Rome: Edizioni Mediterranee.

Goethert, F. W. 1969. "Grabara des Q. Socconius Felix." *Antike Plastik* 9:79–87, pls. 50–56.

Guerrier, Jacqueline. 1980. "Le serviteur à serviette dans la sculpture gallo-romaine." *RAE* 31:231–40.

Herbig, R. 1925. "Mosaik im Casino der Villa Borghese." *MDAI(R)* 40:313–14.

Himmelmann, Nikolaus. 1971. *Archäologisches zum Problem der griechischen Sklaverei.* AbhMainz 1971.13. Wiesbaden: Steiner.

Korać, Miomir. 1991. "Late Roman Tomb with Frescoes from *Viminacium.*" *Starinar* 42:107–22.

Liverani, Paolo. 1988. "Le proprietà private nell'area Lateranense fino all'età di Costantino." *MEFRA* 100:891–915.

Lucot, A., ed. 1912. *Palladius: Histoire Lausiaque.* Paris: A. Picard.

Marchetti, D. 1892. *NSA* 1892:44–48.

Marquardt, Joachim. 1886. *Das Privatleben der Römer.* 2d ed., rev. August Mau. Leipzig: S. Hirzel.

Merlin, Alfred. 1919. "Note sur une mosaïque récemment découverte à Dougga." *BCTH* 1919:3–9, pl. 1.

Mielsch, Harald. 1978. "Zur stadtrömischen Malerei des 4. Jahrhunderts n. Chr." *MDAI(R)* 85:151–207, pls. 80–100.

———. 2001. *Römische Wandmalerei.* Darmstadt: Theiss.

Mundell Mango, Marlia, and Anna Bennett. 1994. *The Sevso Treasure* I. *JRA* Suppl. 12. Ann Arbor.

Nielsen, Hanne Sigismund. 1990. "*Delicia* in Roman Literature and in the Urban Inscriptions." *ARID* 19:79–88.

Nuber, H. U. 1972. "Kanne und Griffschale. Ihr Gebrauch im täglichen Leben und die Beigabe in Gräbern der römischen Kaiserzeit." *BRGK* 53:1–232, pls. 1–31.

Papi, E. 1999. "Schola Praeconum." In *Lexicon Topographicum Urbis Romae,* ed. E. M. Steinby, IV, 254–55. Rome: Quasar.

Peachin, Michael. 2001. "Friendship and Abuse at the Dinner Table." In *Aspects of Friendship in the Greco-Roman World,* ed. M. Peachin. *JRA* Suppl. 43:135–44. Portsmouth RI.

Pelekanidis, Stylianos. 1969. "Die Malerei der konstantinischen Zeit." *Akten des VII. Internationalen Kongresses für christliche Archäologie, Trier 1965:*215–35, pls. 111–130. Vatican City: Pontificio Istituto di Archeologia cristiana; Berlin: Deutsches archäologisches Institut.

Perdrizet, Paul. 1905. "Inscriptions de Salonique." *MEFR* 25:81–95.

Piccottini, Gernot. 1977. *Die Dienerinnen- und Diener-reliefs des Stadtgebietes von Virunum.* CSIR Österreich II.3. Vienna: Österreichische Akademie der Wissenschaften.

Pillinger, Renate, V. Popova, and B. Zimmermann, eds. 1999. *Corpus der spätantiken und frühchristlichen Wandmalereien Bulgariens.* Vienna: Österreichische Akademie der Wissenschaften.

Pirzio Biroli Stefanelli, Lucia. 1991. *L'argento dei Romani: Vasellame da tavola e d'apparato.* Rome: L'Erma di Bretschneider.

Ploumis, Ida. 1997. "Gifts in the Late Roman Iconography." In *Patron and Pavements in Late Antiquity*, ed. Signe Isager and Birte Poulsen. Halicarnassian Studies 2:125–41, pl. 10. Odense: Odense University Press.

Pollini, John. 1999. "The Warren Cup: Homoerotic Love and Symposial Rhetoric in Silver." *ArtB* 81:21–52.

———. 2002. *Gallo-Roman Bronzes and the Process of Romanization: The Cobannus Hoard*. Monumenta Graeca et Romana 9. Leiden: Brill.

Pozzi, Enrica et al. 1986. *Le collezioni del Museo Nazionale di Napoli. I mosaici, le pitture, gli oggetti di uso quotidiano, gli argenti, le terrecotte invetriate, i vetri, i cristalli, gli avori*. Rome: De Luca.

Raeck, Wulf. 1987. "Publica non despiciens. Ergänzungen zur Interpretation des Dominus-Julius-Mosaiks aus Karthago." *MDAI(R)* 94:295–308, pls. 138–39.

Santa Maria Scrinari, Valnea. 1991. *Il Laterano Imperiale. I. Dalle "aedes Laterani" alla "Domus Faustae."* Vatican City: Pontificio Istituto di Archeologia cristiana.

Schäfer, Alfred. 1997. *Unterhaltung beim griechischen Symposion. Darbietungen, Spiele und Wettkämpfe von homerischer bis in spätklassische Zeit*. Mainz: von Zabern.

Schneider, Lambert. 1983. *Die Domäne als Weltbild. Wirkungsstrukturen der spätantiken Bildersprache*. Wiesbaden: Franz Steiner.

Shelton, Kathleen. 1981. *The Esquiline Treasure*. London: British Museum Publications.

———. 1985. "The Esquiline Treasure: The Nature of the Evidence." *AJA* 89:147–55.

Slater, William J. 1974. "Pueri, turba minuta." *BICS* 21:133–40.

Strocka, V. M. 1995. "Tetrarchische Wandmalereien in Ephesos." *Antiquité Tardive* 3:77–89.

Valeva, Julia. 1990. "La signification du cortège représenté dans le tombeau de Silistra. Essai de datation." *Revue Archéologique de Picardie* 1990(1/2):113–16.

———. 2001. "La peinture funéraire dans les provinces orientales de l'empire romain dans l'antiquité tardive." *Hortus Artium Medievalium* 7:167–208.

Veyne, Paul. 1981. "Les cadeaux des colons à leur propriétaire: la neuvième bucolique et le mausolée d'Igel." *RA* 1981.2:245–52.

Warland, Rainer. 1994. "Status und Formular in der Repräsentation der spätantiken Führungsschicht." *MDAI(R)* 101:175–202, pls. 71–75.

Wilpert, Josef. 1903. *Die Malereien der Katakomben Roms*. Freiburg im Br.: Herder.

Wrede, Henning. 1972. *Die spätantike Hermengalerie von Welschbillig*. Berlin: de Gruyter.